MW01291058

JESUS

IN

JACOB

Laying Hold of God and Man

*This book is dedicated to those
who love the study of God's Word
and want to know Him more.
May He come alive to you as never before.*

"If only there were someone to arbitrate between us,
to lay his hand upon us both." - Job 9:33

"A star will come out of Jacob;
a scepter will rise out of Israel."
- Numbers 21:17

Table of Contents

Introduction

Table of Types

Introduction

"So I say to you: Ask and it will be given to you; seek and you will find..." - Luke 11:9

From the moment I first began to develop a relationship with Jesus, I knew a change had taken place inside. Once I began to understand what He had done for me, I knew things would never be the same. It was as though someone had turned the light on and all of a sudden I could see! I could see God. Not literally visually see Him, but all of a sudden God made sense. All of a sudden God became real to me and I wanted to learn and know everything about Him that I possibly could. I began to see everything revolved around Him and was for His glory.

In the beginning, however, I could never have anticipated that my initial sense of discovery would last for years, as an ongoing enlightenment that would lead me throughout my Christian journey. With every step and every turn I continue to see God in a new light. Twenty-two years later I am still discovering subtle nuances and facets of His character and how He operates. Today, I'm amazed at how I can look at what are normal everyday experiences and if I take the time and if I choose to look deeper I can see Jesus in them. After all, He does say, "If we seek, we will find." I believe that if we seek, we will find it to be true that, "All things were created by him and for him. He is before all things, and in him *all things* hold together" (Colossians 1:16-17). Certainly, if all things are held together in Him, there is at least the possibility for us to see Him in all things.

Oh, how it helps to see Jesus. It helps to see Him in the daily events of life that we all have to go through. It helps to see

1

Him in each and every circumstance. When we look past the natural, the temporal, and the physical, to see Jesus with eyes of faith, it just makes everything worthwhile. It makes everything all right. It brings peace to the storm, sight to blind eyes, light into darkness, and joy to despair.

The old hymn says, "When we all see Jesus we'll sing and shout the victory." Well, I don't know about you, but I don't want to have to wait for the full future manifestation of heaven to experience victory. This can be a present, everyday reality as I see Jesus even in the least of these (Matthew 25:40).

1 John 3:2-3 says, "But we know that when he appears, we shall be like him, for we shall see him as he is. Everyone who has this hope in him purifies himself, just as he is pure." It is when we see Him that we will be changed to be like Him. This text is referring to the full consummation of Christians ultimately being conformed to the image of Christ upon seeing Him at His Second Coming. However, I want to state again that by faith you can see Him now. Yes it's true, now we only see in part (I Corinthians 13:9-12), but the more we do see of Him, the more we will want to conform to His image and be like Him.

I want to see more of the Lord now! I'm on a quest to find, to see, and to know Jesus. I know that if I can see Him a little more clearly, I'll love Him even more dearly.

As I have embarked on this frontier I have found that the easiest place to find Jesus is in the God-breathed, Holy Spirit inspired Scriptures. Jesus said in John 5:39-40, "You diligently study the Scriptures because you think that by them you possess eternal life. These are the Scriptures that testify about me."

Now, of course, the Scriptures Jesus was referring to at the time were the Old Testament texts. Both Old and New Covenants

2

testify of Jesus, but the verse here in John chapter 5 specifically shows that the Old Covenant holds an important role in testifying to Jesus being the Messiah. Hallelujah, He's all through the Scriptures!

In the Old Covenant, Jesus had not yet physically manifested in the flesh. He did, however, reveal Himself. I, along with many Bible teachers, believe He appeared in the Old Testament in angelic form. He appeared as The Angel of the Lord to Hagar, Moses, Balaam, Joshua, Gideon, and others. Note that in all these and other references He is referred to as, "*The* Angel of the Lord" and not *an* angel of the Lord.

More often than His appearances as "The Angel of the Lord" however, are the subtle references to Him manifested through foreshadows, types and figures. These are similarities between Christ and events, people, or objects in the Old Covenant texts. Just as easily as Jesus can be seen foreshadowed in the Old Covenant, we can also see types of fallen man, the Church, the Trinity, and even types of the spiritual battles we all face in our New Testament Christian walk.

Speaking of Old Testament events, Paul writes in 1 Corinthians 10:11, "These things happened to them as *examples* and were written down as warnings for us, on whom the fulfillment of the ages has come." Old Testament characters and events are outward physical examples of what we now know as fulfilled inward spiritual realities in the New Testament.

So, here we are. We're on a quest to find Jesus in the life of Jacob. Some will say, "Surely, with the character flaws and reputation of this man we wouldn't be able to find anything in common with Christ. Surely, we couldn't use the 'trickster' Jacob to draw parallels with Jesus." Or, could we?

3

Understandably, to find Jesus in Jacob we will have to overcome some hurdles. Jacob has been labeled a swindler, a cheat, a supplanter, a deceiver, and a thief. On these grounds many have disqualified him and would never attempt to look at Jacob to find Jesus. In fact, Jacob has been used as a prime example of God's grace toward sinful man. Truly, Jacob was not perfect and was an object of God's grace as we all are. I do not want to minimize that message. I do believe, however, that over the course of time Jacob has gotten the short end of the stick. I believe he has been mislabeled by many theologians and has something more to offer. Ultimately, no matter what you, or me, or the greatest of scholars think, God's fair and just position still remains, *"Jacob I loved, but Esau I hated"* (Romans 9:13).

As you join me on this journey to find Jesus in the life of the long misunderstood patriarch Jacob, allow the Holy Spirit to shed light on previously hidden types and shadows so His glory may be more fully known.

ONE

Typical Typology

"You diligently study the Scriptures because you think that by them you possess eternal life. These are the Scriptures that testify about me." - John 5:39-40

Typology is the study of types. Types are foreshadowings that point to a greater future fulfillment. There are types in the Old Covenant, which develop beautiful pictures of what ultimately has been revealed in the New Covenant through Christ. These pictures are imbedded throughout the text, and they're obvious once brought to light. However, a type should not be seen as the primary interpretation of any text. Scripture is always to be interpreted literally except where it is obvious that a figure of speech is being used. As we consider the typological treatment of texts, we need to view any type that may become apparent as an additional secondary abstraction underlying the Scripture. When it comes to types and foreshadows, that is exactly what they are. Do not make them anything more. The misuse of types and shadows to develop principles that are contradictory to sound biblical interpretation should not and cannot be tolerated. The purpose of this typological study is to only accentuate and confirm truths that are already proven from the full counsel of the Word of God. The primary purpose of this study is to develop a picture, not a doctrine.

Also, when dealing with types, we must not force every Old Covenant revelation to be a foreshadowing nor should we try to make every aspect of our New Covenant reality fit perfectly into an Old Covenant type. Again, the definition of a type is a figure, representation, symbol, or foreshadowing of something to come. Types and shadows are not perfect parallels and they eventually break down. Jacob was a real historic person who lived about 2,000 years before Jesus. Jacob was not Jesus. Jacob's physical father was Isaac, not God. Isaac died, God cannot. Jacob was not perfect; Jesus was perfect, and so on. Every consideration will not fit perfectly, but I believe you'll be amazed at how much Jesus you can see as we look at the Scriptural account of Jacob.

Another point I need to make is that on an academic level some may consider the similarities between Jacob and Jesus analogies rather than types. I am not inclined to dissect the differences between the two in this presentation, but I am willing to say that assessment is certainly possible. In fact, types many times contain analogies. My goal is not for this to strictly be a typological study per se; instead, it is my desire to find Christ in the Old Covenant text. If you would rather refer to the similarities presented in this study as analogies, by all means do; just don't miss the similarities. For the remainder of the study I will continue referring to the Old Covenant snapshots of our Redeemer as types and foreshadows and leave the exact definitions and which category they fall into to scholars and time.

Lastly, before I lay out the typological context for Jacob, let me present a number of the more accepted and traditional types from the Old Covenant. This is a very broad stroke of the brush to put us in a typological mind set. Some examples include: Jonah's time in the belly of a fish as a type of Jesus' time in the grave. Matthew 12:40 says, "For as Jonah was three days and three nights in the belly of a huge fish, so the Son of Man will be three days and three nights in the heart of the earth." The account of Abraham sacrificing his son Isaac is often used as a type of the Father sacrificing His Son Jesus. Joseph, being thrown into a pit

6

and subsequently being raised to rule over Egypt, as well as other aspects of Joseph's life, are used as types of Christ. The brazen serpent of Numbers 21:9 is a type of Jesus being lifted up on the cross. John 3:14-15 says, "Just as Moses lifted up the snake in the desert, so the Son of Man must be lifted up, that everyone who believes in him may have eternal life." The Passover is a beautiful type of Christ according to 1 Corinthians 5:7, which says, "Christ our Passover is sacrificed for us." Melchizedek, the high priest, the tabernacle, as well as the entire sacrificial system is seen as a type according to Hebrews chapters 7 through 9. Jesus can be seen all through the Old Covenant if you look for Him.

Now, let's begin focusing on the specific context that sets the stage for Jacob. The context in which we find ourselves is the book of Genesis, the book of beginnings. "In the beginning God created." He created Adam, whose name came to generically represent man but literally means "red" because he was created from the red dust of the earth. Later in this study we will see that Edom, which also means "red" is another name used by Jacob's brother Esau. Both men, Adam and Edom, despised their birthright.

Adam had both a "Cain" and an "Abel" within his loins. Typologically, Adam represents man and he had within him both a Cain, who represents the flesh and an Abel who represents the spirit. Cain literally means "to acquire" or "a spear" while Abel means, "breath" or "vapor." *Cain/flesh* prevailed and killed *Abel/spirit*. Therefore, *Cain/flesh* was cursed by God and driven from the land of delight (Eden) and eternal life. Then Adam had a third son, Seth.

It's interesting that even though Adam probably had many more sons and daughters, only three are mentioned. I believe only three are mentioned for instructional purposes. The picture here is a picture of the man "Adam," producing man. Although man is not divine like God, he has been made in the image of God and is in many respects *triune* in nature. Man is made of three parts, which can be separated into spirit, soul, and body.

The name Seth, according to Easton's Bible Dictionary, means: appointed or a substitute. His mother gave him this name, "for God," she said, "hath appointed me another *seed* instead of Abel, whom Cain slew" (Genesis 4:25 KJV).

Seth (an appointed substitute), like we'll find in Jacob, is also a picture of Jesus. Ultimately, Jesus was the appointed substitute who lived the *spirit/Abel* filled life we could not. Our *spirit/Abel* is dead because of the prevailing corruption of our *flesh/Cain*, so our spirit needs to be born again through *Christ Jesus/Seth*.

Luke 3:38 shows us that Jesus can be traced back through the line of Seth. The line or lineage of growth this "seed" generated can actually be seen through both Luke's genealogy of Mary and Matthew's genealogy of Jesus' earthly stepfather, Joseph. Seth, then, was indeed the "seed" that contained and produced the kingly Davidic line, which ultimately resulted in the manifestation of the King of kings, our Lord Jesus. In other words, the appointed substitute produced the Appointed Substitute. The "seed" of Seth produced the "Seed" of Jesus (Galatians 3:16), who would ultimately produce the spiritual family God desired.

The next main type we see in the book of Genesis is Noah. Noah delivered his family (all who got into the ark) out of the water. He can be viewed as a foreshadowing of both Moses and John the Baptist, while the universal flood can symbolize baptism (1 Peter 3:20-21). "Moses" means "from out of the water," and he delivered his people out of Egypt by passing through the Sea (water). John the Baptist's baptism of course, was a baptism of water also. And yes, all who respond to John's baptism of

8

repentance and turn to Jesus will be saved!

Next, in the 12th chapter of Genesis, we come to a point where God begins to work specifically through three men theologians call Patriarchs. Patriarch simply means, "Father." Note again, there are three men who are referred to by this term. Man is triune because we were made in God's image. "Let *us* make man in *our* image" (Genesis 1:26). We serve a God who is three and yet one. He is one God, but yet He is Father, Son, and Holy Spirit. This is what theologians call the *Trinity*.

The three fathers are: Abraham, Isaac, and Jacob. I see the three of them individually and collectively as a picture of God. All arc fathers (God) with Abraham being the head father of our faith, (the Father). In fact, Abraham's name literally means, "father of a multitude."

I think it is appropriate that Abraham, our father of faith and a type of Father God, dealt with the *promise* that he would become a father. In 2 Corinthians 1:20 it says, "For no matter how many *promises* God has made, they are 'Yes' in Christ." It is God, the Father, who makes the promises and sends forth the Word. It is the Father who "wills." It is *Jesus/Jacob* who then fulfills the Father's will and promises. "Do not leave Jerusalem, but wait for the gift my *Father promised*" (Acts 1:4).

Next there is Isaac, who represents the Holy Spirit. His name means "laughter" which can be paralleled with the joy we're to receive in the Holy Ghost (Romans 14:17). It is also interesting that Isaac is the least mentioned of the three, yet it is through him that Jacob, a type of Jesus, is born. The angel said to Mary in Luke 1:35-36, "The Holy Spirit will come upon you, and the power of the Most High will overshadow you. So the holy one to be born will be called the Son of God." Also in regards to Isaac, we will see that he is associated with prayer. It is appropriate he deals with prayer for that is what the Holy Spirit does. Romans 8:26-27 tells us, "In the same way, the Spirit helps us in our weakness. We do not know what we ought to pray for, but the Spirit himself intercedes for us with groans that words cannot express." The Holy Spirit empowers and prays.

Then, appropriately, we have Jacob, a type of Jesus, who persevered. Jesus, with much prayer and the empowerment of the Holy Spirit, persevered to accomplish the will and promises of the Father. Hebrews 12:2 shows us that Jesus, "the author and perfecter of our faith, who for the joy set before him *endured* the cross." Ultimately, out of Jacob came twelve sons who were the beginning of the nation of Israel. Likewise, we have the Son Jesus, out of who came, "a chosen people, a royal priesthood, *a holy nation*, a people belonging to God" (1 Peter 2:9). And likewise, this nation also began with twelve chosen "sons" called "apostles" (sent ones).

Now, I know this is a broad sweep, but it's starting to get good already. You see, there could have been two patriarchs. There could have been four, five or six, but there aren't. There are three, just three. Of course, the exclusive recognition of three patriarchs is not because of Judaism. Jewish rabbis do not recognize the Godhead Trinity. No, it's God who continually chooses to be known as the God of Abraham, Isaac and Jacob. I believe that our One True and Sovereign Triune God inspired writers to reveal His will and nature through Scripture exactly how He determined. And, I believe along with Jesus, that the Scriptures (on many levels) testify of Him!

TWO

Pregnant through Prayer

"The LORD answered his prayer, and his wife Rebekah became pregnant." - Genesis 25:21

Prayer is communication with God. It is the means through which heaven and earth co-mingle. Prayer, however, does not change God. It changes us. God works and molds the heart of a person who prays. Something always has to happen in us before it can happen through us. In Genesis 25:21 where the study of Jacob officially begins, *"Isaac prayed* to the LORD on behalf of his wife, because she was barren. *The LORD answered* his prayer, and his wife *Rebekah became pregnant."*

Before I make a couple of points specific to prayer, allow me to make another broad typological claim regarding barrenness.

If you flip back a few chapters in Genesis you'll find in Genesis 16:1 that Abram's wife Sarai had also been barren. Now in chapter 25 Isaac's wife Rebekah is barren and then finally in Genesis 29:31 we will learn that Jacob's wife Rachel was also barren. Is this possibly a coincidence? Certainly not with God!

If Abraham, Isaac, and Jacob are a type of the Trinity, then their brides can be viewed as a type of Israel and/or the Church. Notice though, in each case it is not the bridegroom, but the bride who is barren. It was not Abraham, Isaac, nor Jacob who were

11

impotent and we certainly know God is not impotent. No, each time it is the desired and beloved bride who is barren.

Now, let me briefly mention the exception of Rachel's older sister, Leah. Laban, Jacob's father-in-law, surprisingly gave Leah to be Jacob's wife before he gave his younger daughter and the apple of Jacob's eye, Rachel. Leah was *"not loved,"* but she was the first to naturally bear offspring without any prerequisites other than having relations with Jacob. Genesis 29:31 says, "When the LORD saw that Leah was not loved, he opened her womb, but Rachel was barren."

It is not until Jacob (our type of Jesus) has union with the one who was "not loved" that fruit was naturally and freely allowed to come forth. The "not loved" Leah, will be used later in this study as a type of the gentiles who were afar off and alienated from God. You and I both know that we, as the bride, come before Him barren and unable to yield fruit in and of ourselves. It is only through our union with *Jesus/Jacob* that we will ever bring forth that which He desires.

But wait. Some will argue that Sarai had union with Abraham who's a type of Father God, but she remained barren for years. Typologically, upon having union with *Abraham / the Father* why didn't she immediately and naturally begin to produce?

It seems it is because the primary lesson we learn from the life of Abraham is the lesson of faith, particularly faith in God's Word or faith in His Promise. So, even though she had relations with Abraham, she had to remain barren for a season to allow room for faith to be demonstrated. Ultimately, however, the promise she and Abraham had believed came to pass when she bore the fruit of a newborn Isaac!

Well, what about Rebekah? She had union with her husband Isaac (a type of the Holy Spirit) and she didn't initially produce either. If Isaac were a type of the Holy Spirit, wouldn't Rebekah (or anyone) have immediately been productive upon entering into that union? Unfortunately, I know a number of Christians who have the Holy Spirit living inside them, but they're not very productive for the Kingdom. That would all change though, if they would just begin to pray. You have to remember, after prayer Rebekah did bear fruit! And for us too, it will require praying in the Spirit in order to bear the fruit of the Spirit.

Then what about Jacob? Although Leah (gentiles) began to produce first, ultimately Rachel (Israel) did also, and the only reason either of them were productive was because *Jesus/Jacob* persevered and fulfilled the demands of Laban, whom we will see later is a type of the Law.

Oh, it's so incredibly beautiful how God has intricately woven Himself into the fabric of the masterpiece of His own revealed Word!

Now let's make this personal. Do you want to produce good fruit in keeping with repentance? Do you want to bear Galatians chapter 5 spiritual fruit? Then each of us must have faith in God's promises, pray, and most definitely persevere, because each of these will cause us to be productive. Faith and perseverance along with prayer are each a cure for spiritual barrenness, but here in our text we are looking specifically at Isaac, his prayer, and what prayer can do. Prayer is powerful. We need to pray like Isaac prayed. We need to pray that the Bride be fruitful. If you and I want to be productive rather than barren, we have to pray! If you want a dream or a vision, if you want to walk in the anointing and have power in your life, if you want to bear good fruit, then you need to pray! If you want to be like Jesus, you must pray!

Genesis 25:21 says, "Isaac prayed to the LORD on behalf of his wife because she was barren."

Husbands you need to pray for your wives. Isaac prayed for Rebekah. You also need to bring your wife before the Lord. Pray about her needs and her desires. And, not only do you need to pray for her, you need to pray with her. Jesus prays for His Bride (Romans 8:32), but He's asked us as His Bride to pray along with Him also. I believe Jesus loves it when His Bride comes into agreement with Him in praying the will of the Father. If it's good enough for Jesus, then it's certainly good enough for you and me!

To wrap up this section on becoming pregnant by prayer, I want to add two additional instances where godly men were literally born because of prayer. First, there was John the Baptist. His mother Elizabeth was also barren until the angel came to her husband Zechariah and told him, "Do not be afraid, Zechariah; *your prayer has been heard.* Your wife Elizabeth will bear you a son, and you are to give him the name John." This event again establishes my unwavering belief that the only way to get God results is by going to God.

The second example is found in I Samuel 1:7. "It happened *year after year*, as often as she went up to the house of the LORD, she would provoke her; so she wept and would not eat." And then in verses 12-13, "Now it came about, as she *continued praying* before the LORD, that Eli was watching her mouth. As for Hannah, she was speaking in her heart, only her lips were moving, but her voice was not heard. So, Eli thought she was drunk."

Hannah continued year after year to go up to the house of the Lord to pray that she would have a child. Finally her prayer manifested in the form of her son, Samuel the prophet. The name Samuel literally means, "heard of God."

Like Hannah, do not fear what others might think. Do not give up on getting results. When you pray, do not quit. Do not stop praying until the manifestation is realized in your life. Pray, pray, and then pray some more! Ask and keep on asking, seek and keep on seeking, knock and keep on knocking until the door is opened to you. Also, contrary to some teaching, it is not Scriptural to pray only one time and never bring up the issue to God again. Some feel it shows a lack of faith if you have to pray about something more than once. True biblical faith, however, keeps on praying until what the Spirit has placed in you is brought to fruition. According to the account of the persistent widow in Luke 18:1-8, Jesus wants you to be persistent in your prayers. Allow the divine impartation of God's will to be conceived in you through prayer and then keep on praying through!

THREE

Carrying a Struggle

"For in my inner being I delight in God's law; but I see another law at work in the members of my body, waging war against the law of my mind..." - Romans 7:22-23

"Isaac prayed to the LORD on behalf of his wife, because she was barren. The LORD answered his prayer, and his wife Rebekah became pregnant. *The babies jostled each other within her,* and she said, 'Why is this happening to me?' So she went to inquire of the LORD" (Genesis 25:21-22).

Have you ever struggled about how to deal with a situation? Have you ever wrestled with which decision to make, or what direction to go in? Have you ever known what needed to be done, but weren't sure how to go about it? This is the struggle inherent in everything God has for you. This was the struggle for Adam and now the two trees in the garden are in you. Both the bride and the harlot are in you. Wheat and tares coexist. Both Jacob and Esau jostle inside. You can try to get where God wants you to go by either partaking of the tree of the knowledge of good and evil or by partaking of the Tree of Life. You can prepare yourself as a Bride or commit adultery with the world. You can choose the Jacob route or the Esau way. "I have set before you life and death, blessings and curses. Now choose life" (Deuteronomy 30:19).

Once you have received a divine impartation by the Spirit, you must then carry that gift to term by the Spirit. Unfortunately, many times the Spirit of God places a dream, a gift, a vision, a ministry, or an anointing in a person, but instead of allowing proper incubation and nourishment by the Spirit, the birth is prematurely brought about in the flesh. Moses killing the Egyptian in Exodus 2:12 is a good example of this. God wanted Moses to rule and judge His people, but when and how Moses went about it was premature. The wrestling for dominance between the flesh and the Spirit is what we see taking place inside of Rebekah. There's a jostling going on inside her between Esau who represents the flesh, and Jacob who represents Jesus, or the Spirit-led man.

It's wonderful when the Spirit conceives a dream, vision, or ministry in you. But it has to be brought to term by the Spirit also.

The devil will try to use the weakness of your flesh in one of two ways. First, he'll try to make you rashly react entirely engaging in the appetites of the flesh. Blatant moral failure and a focus on the flesh to this degree will cause the neglect of necessary spiritual nourishment. A prodigal move such as this will ultimately abort the vision the Spirit originally gave. If, however, the devil cannot get you to outright terminate your dream or vision, the more subtle second temptation is to entice you to continue bringing the spiritual goal to fruition, but to do it according to the works of the flesh rather than being led by the Lord. This strategy keeps you thinking you're in the will of God, but the truth is, you are really relying on your own ability to make God's will happen. The correct process is, "not by might, nor by power but *by my Spirit* says the Lord" (Zechariah 4:6).

The struggle I'm referring to is the primary struggle within each Christian. It is the struggle between flesh and spirit. Before someone becomes a Christian the struggle isn't there. A non-Christian is completely flesh dominated with no opposition. The spirit has not come alive within the non-Christian. But, once a person is born again by the Spirit, they no longer have to be dominated by their flesh and a battle ensues. The apostle Paul aptly describes this struggle in Romans chapter seven. The question is; which will dominate in you?

Rebekah's response to the jostling within her was to once again, pray. As we covered in the last chapter prayer will impregnate you, but you then need to *continue* praying. When you don't know what to do, pray! When you want to know why what's happening to you, is happening to you, pray! When you need victory over the flesh, pray! Rebekah went to inquire of the Lord.

The Lord answered Rebekah. But, His response might not have been what Rebekah expected. The Lord didn't tell her He would cause the fighting and jostling inside her to subside. God didn't tell her to dip seven times in the Jordan and the babies would be at peace. God didn't tell her to put mud on her belly, wash herself in the pool of Siloam and the babies would stop fighting. No, He didn't say He would stop the struggle, but He did give her a Word that brought understanding.

I don't know about you, but sometimes even if my circumstances don't change, I can cope with them much better if I simply know what's going on. If you will just help me understand what's really happening, then I can handle whatever it is I'm dealing with.

It's like the contractor who should have started my job two weeks ago. If he would call and simply explain why he hasn't started the job yet, then I can reason it through and possibly consider alternate plans. But at least, he's given me opportunity to evaluate his excuse.

If he simply keeps me in the loop, then I can handle what's happening to a greater degree. On the other hand, if day after day he continues to not show up and he doesn't let me know what's going on, then it won't be long before I get someone else to do the work he's not doing.

God understands this about us and He wants us to be in the loop (John 15:15). He wants us to know what He is doing. He still may let us go through the circumstance, but He knows the only way we're going to learn from the experience is for us to know why we had to go through it to begin with.

"Lord, just give me a word on it; just give me insight; a revelation." If I have God's Word on it, I can handle anything! Getting a Word about your situation can almost be as encouraging as getting the manifestation itself. And, when it's a Word from God it's certainly as sure. Really, you can take His Word on it!

It is also true, however, that sometimes carrying what God has given you can become an exasperating and frustrating season. The struggle between the flesh and the Spirit to manifest what God has placed in you can grow wearisome. Have you ever wished that dream inside would just happen so you could see it, hold it, and handle it? But, as the old saying goes, "good things come to those who wait." So what you need to do in the waiting is get a Word. Stand on God's Word and allow God to work. Scripture says, in Isaiah 55:11 that *His word will not return void.*

Many times it is only after you combine the gift God has placed in you (a dream, a vision, a ministry, a desire of the heart) with a specific Word from God about that gift, and you learn to cherish each of them as much as the fruition itself that God then causes the gift to manifest.

20

The possibility of bringing forth what God has placed in you either by the Spirit or by the flesh is a struggle each of us carries. Carry it knowing the flesh will bear flesh and the Spirit will bear Spirit; choose the Spirit.

FOUR

My, What Big Babies
You Have

"For as in Adam all die, so in Christ all will be made alive."
- 1 Corinthians 15:22

Once God has given you a gift to carry, you then have to have a proper understanding of the sheer immensity and impact the flesh and/or Spirit can have.

"The LORD said to her, '*Two nations are in your womb*, and two peoples from within you will be separated; one people will be stronger than the other, and the older will serve the younger'" (Genesis 25:23).

I was an eight pound fifteen ounce baby and my brother was ten pounds when he was born. By most standards we were both pretty good size newborns. But, we didn't even begin to compare to what Rebekah had. Our text tells us that two nations were in her womb. Now of course, she didn't literally, materially, physically at that moment have two entire nations within her. But you have to remember who's giving the word. This is God. When God speaks, He just as easily speaks from our future as our present because it's all now for Him. He's already been to our future, knows it, worked it out, and simultaneously guides us into what He's planned. Oh, it's a great thing to put your trust in the One who *is* (present tense) the Alpha and Omega and everything in between.

Too many times we minimize the gift, the vision, and even the Holy Ghost Himself whom God has placed inside of us. I believe God has nations inside of you. God has great big dreams, hopes, and plans that He wants to bring forth from within you. God wants to produce world-impacting things through your life! They may seem small now, but if it's God, and you allow it to continue to be God, then great things are possible.

You must realize the importance of what God has placed in you; that ministry, that desire in your heart, that vision, that fire that cannot be quenched... That's God and it's not a small insignificant thing. It's incredible! It's awesome! It's huge!

You have to stop viewing it as if, "oh, it's nothing." You have to stop thinking, "Oh, anyone can do it." That's not so! Not anyone can do it. And, they certainly can't do it like you can. God placed it in you for you to deliver. Carry it with compassion. Carry it with fear and trembling and work it out of you - Yes, even the fullness of your salvation! Let what is in you come out and when you do wait and see. It's going to be BIG.

"Nations are in your womb!"

You might think you are simply showing love to that one child, but God sees all those whom that child is going to impact because of what you meant to him. You think you are just being kind to your neighbor, but God sees how they will reach thousands. You think you started that small storefront church and you wonder what kind of influence you are having. But, God sees the rippling effect of His word that does not return void and how it will cover the earth as the waters cover the sea.

Okay, you're beginning to understand how big this baby is when it's God and you allow God to bring it forth. But what about the flesh? How big can a baby get when it's brought forth in the flesh? It can't be that big of a deal, can it?

All I have to say about the negative ramifications of the flesh is look at the size of today's problems brought about by Adam just one time despising his birthright by eating of the tree of the knowledge of good and evil. Look at the Ishmael size problems in the world today because Abraham tried to bring about the Promise of the Spirit (Isaac/Jacob) by the arm of the flesh (Ishmael/Esau).

Yes, Adam's sin and Ishmael's false religion are both big fleshy babies, but praise God our text tells us the younger spiritual *Jesus/Jacob* is stronger! Genesis 25:23 says, "One people will be stronger than the other, and the older will serve the younger."

Along with the sheer immensity of potential for each gift that is in you, as I mentioned in the previous chapter, each gift also comes with its own innate struggle. There will always be a struggle within you to make what God has for you come to pass in your own strength or by trusting God to bring it about in His time and by His power. The gift in you can manifest either as a Jacob or an Esau.

Let me tell you here, God loves to be the one who makes it happen. Remember, *God loves Jacob, but He hates Esau.* God always works through and for His promise.

Also, as our text states, there will always be a separation between the two and one will be stronger than the other. I guarantee God wants the older to serve the younger. God wants Esau to serve Jacob. God wants your flesh to submit to Jesus. Once you are born again and become a "*new* creature" in Christ,

God wants your *old* man to die. The old way of being, the old fleshly way of accomplishing things must come into submission to the younger, spiritual *Jesus/Jacob* way. If you keep the old wineskin way of doing things you will ruin it all, but if you replace the old with new skins, you will be able to expand and contain the new things God is wanting for your life (Matthew 9:16,17).

Again, Genesis 25:23 says, "Two nations are in your womb, and two peoples from within you *will be separated*; one people will be stronger than the other, and the *older* will *serve* the *younger*."

Both the flesh and the Spirit want to manifest the dreams and desires that God has placed in you. You will, knowingly or unknowingly, choose one and thereby separate yourself from the other. You will either sow to the flesh and reap the large-scale impact of the destruction thereof, or you will sow to the Spirit and reap the huge harvest of eternal life. Now you have a decision to make. Which will you feed? Which will you cater to? Which will you sow to? The one you emphasize and spend time with will be the one that becomes bigger and stronger in your life. If you feed the flesh you will separate yourself from the Spirit. On the other hand, if you choose to sow to the Spirit you will automatically begin to separate from the desires of the flesh. Which nation (kingdom) do you want to flourish?

"No one can serve two masters. Either he will hate the one and love the other, or he will be devoted to the one and despise the other" (Matthew 6:24).

You see, the one you love the most is the one you'll serve. And, the one you serve is the one who has mastery over you. If you like the ways of the flesh, then you will serve it. If you prefer the ways of God, you will serve Him. Jacob or Esau—who is stronger in you?

"When the time came for her to give birth, there were twin boys in her womb" (Genesis 25:24).

Rebekah had twins. These twins, Jacob and Esau, were obviously fraternal rather than identical twins. Really, outside of the birth experience, they had very little in common. Their lives were probably as different as an unsaved individual who merely tries to survive in the world after physical birth and the abundant life of significance and purpose a Christian has after he or she has experienced spiritual rebirth. One had a narrow focus seeing no value of investing into something beyond instant gratification and the other had a big picture view toward eternity.

Let me highlight a few distinctions the text brings out between these two nations.

> The first to come out was *red*, and his whole body was like a *hairy garment*; so they named him *Esau*. After this, his brother came out, with his hand *grasping Esau's heel*; so he was named *Jacob*. Isaac was sixty years old when Rebekah gave birth to them. The boys grew up, and Esau became a skillful hunter, a man of the open country, while Jacob was a *quiet* man, staying among the tents. Isaac, who had a taste for wild game, loved Esau, but Rebekah loved Jacob (Genesis 25:25-26).

#1. **Esau (a type of Adam, fallen man, the flesh):** **Name literally means "hairy." Also named Edom, which like the name Adam means "red." Foretold he would have to serve Jacob. God hated Esau. Isaac preferred him.**
> **Physical traits:** Red hair, hairy garment (a covering like an animal), man of the open field, [the field is a type of the world, (Mt. 13:38)] – man of the *world*, a skilled hunter,

27

"hunter" is always used in a negative light in Scripture (Nimrod was another hunter: Nimrod means *"rebel"*)

Character traits: Impulsive, short sighted, wanted instant gratification, quick (hasty) decisions, made things happen himself, despised the valuable and eternal, gives up, sells out, loses the birthright and blessing, vengeful.

#2.   Jacob (a type of Jesus): Name literally means, "heel grasper."   Foretold he would become lord over brother(s) (plural) (Genesis 27:29). God loved Jacob. Rebekah preferred Jacob.

> **Physical traits:** Smooth skinned, plain man – the Hebrew word for *plain* is *"tam,"* which also means *perfect, upright, and undefiled.* He was quiet and stayed among the tents.
>
> **Character traits:** Opportunistic, appreciated worth, recognized lasting value, obedient, holds on and doesn't let go, fights for the eternal, endures, overcomes, has dreams and communicates with God, gains the birthright and blessing.

Note the combination of Isaac and Rebekah together as husband and wife (one flesh), preferred and wanted the twin combination of both Esau and Jacob (together as one) to succeed. The success of Adam *and* Jesus, the flesh *and* the spirit, the body *and* the head is the desired outcome. *Isaac/God* really loves Esau, but because Esau despised his birthright and sinned, God must "hate" him [the sin of the flesh (Esau)]. I will develop this later. At this point, I simply want to introduce the thought of Isaac and Rebekah as being *"one"* because they are husband and wife (Genesis 2:24).

Typologically, *Esau/Adam* needed a red (blood had to be shed) hairy covering. "The LORD God made garments of skin for Adam and his wife and clothed them" (Genesis 3:21). Jacob, on the other hand, had smooth skin (Genesis 27:11). He had no need for the covering of animals for himself, but *Jesus/Jacob* put on a goatskin covering to become like his brother *Esau/Adam*. And, likewise, Jesus put on red flesh and came as *Esau/Adam*. He came looking like one who needed a covering when in fact He needed none for Himself. *Jesus/Jacob* was an upright *(tam)* man.

I also think it's interesting the text associates Jacob with tents. Tents represent the temporal. Jacob must have associated with them enough for him to realize this wasn't home and that he was just passing through. He must have understood the things of this world are temporary, while the things of God are permanent and lasting. He obviously learned the difference. I guess if we could discern between the two, we wouldn't hold so tightly to the momentary and fleeting, but we, like Jacob, would do whatever we could to gain the eternal; at least I would!

For those of you who are partial to numerology, Isaac was *sixty* when the twins (representing both the flesh and the Spirit-led man) were born. Sixty is six times ten. Six is traditionally known as the number for man. Man was created on the sixth day. The number ten represents universal and perfected completeness (Ten Commandments, ten plagues, the tithe "tenth" represented the whole). Put them together and you get a "whole man." When you have both Esau and Jacob together you get man perfectly or completely "complete." Yes, man has to be born of the flesh *(Esau)*, but to be completely complete; he has to be born of the Spirit *(Jacob)* also.

The story of Jacob and Esau will now begin going into great detail about what must happen for you and I to become the complete person God intends for us to be.

FIVE

Heel Grasper

"After this, his brother came out, with his hand grasping Esau's heel; so he was named Jacob." - Genesis 25:26

While playing a football game during my junior year in high school my ankle rolled as I was tackled by opposing players. The pain was excruciating. I didn't know if it was a bad sprain or broken. I only knew I couldn't walk on it. On the sideline I grabbed the base of my calf squeezing it, trying to give some support and relief to the injury. The trainers iced and then wrapped it. It turned out I had partially ruptured my Achilles tendon, which connects the heel to the calf. I babied that ankle for months before I could run on it again.

I tell this to illustrate that in my pain I needed help. My ankle needed to be treated and cared for. The trainers had to ice and wrap it. I needed help to relieve the pain so I could walk again. This too is exactly what Jesus did for us. He covered and tended our injury.

Genesis 25:25-26 says, "The first to come out was red, and his whole body was like a hairy garment; so they named him Esau. After this, his brother came out, with his hand *grasping Esau's heel*; so he was named Jacob."

I find it interesting that as Esau and Jacob are being birthed, Jacob is grasping the heel of Esau. He could have been grabbing

Esau's leg; his foot, his toe, or he could have not had hold of Esau at all. The very important point, however, is that he did have hold of Esau and it was his *heel* that he was grabbing.

Esau, remember, is a type of the flesh, but more broadly he is also a type of fallen man in Adam. Adam's name means "red" while Esau was literally red haired and called Edom, which also means "red." Typologically then, we have a picture of Jesus holding onto *Adam/fallen man* by the heel. Why is this significant?

Genesis 3:14-15 tells us,

So the LORD God said to the serpent, 'Because you have done this, Cursed are you above all the livestock and all the wild animals! You will crawl on your belly and you will eat dust all the days of your life. And I will put enmity between you and the woman, and between *your offspring and hers*; he will crush your head, and *you will strike his heel*'.

God cursed satan by saying his head would be crushed by the offspring of woman. This is a Messianic reference to Jesus, born of a woman, triumphing over the devil. It also says, however, that satan would strike the heel of the offspring of the woman. Certainly, one interpretation of this "strike on the heel" of man refers to the suffering, which Christ underwent on our behalf prior to and during His crucifixion. There is however, another possible meaning to this "strike on the heel." It could also refer to the continual pain, suffering, and death that man (the offspring of woman) has experienced since Adam sinned by succumbing to the temptation (the bite) of the serpent. Christ's specific "strike on the heel" was the substitute for the universal "strike on the heel" that all mankind has suffered.

Let me ask you a question. If a snake bit your heel, where would you grab? Exactly! You would immediately grab hold of your heel. This is the picture that is developing. Jesus has grabbed hold of and covered the hurt, the pain, and the death the serpent inflicted by striking *Adam/Esau/fallen man*. Although *Esau/fallen man* wanted to be first, wanted to do things his way, wanted instant gratification – still Jesus would not let go. Jesus has held on to man. He could have given up, wiped man off the face of the planet and started over. He could have let go of man and let him desperately falter and flounder in his own sin. But instead, He so embraced man that He became the Son of man. *Jesus came to heal the heel of man.* Not only does He destroy the devil, but He also heals the wounds caused by the devil. There is no longer any sting from the strike. No longer is there any pain from the bite. No longer is there any death from the sin. Jesus has covered and healed the hurting heel of man.

Because He has healed me, I can walk the way I am supposed to. Now, I can bear the weight. Now, I can press on toward the things of God. The Healer has tended to my injury and will not let me go until I'm perfected in Him.

The apostle Paul writes, "I press on to take hold of that for which *Christ Jesus took hold of me*" (Philippians 3:12).

Indeed He did take hold of us, to the point of becoming like us. "Since the children have flesh and blood, he too shared in their humanity so that by his death he might destroy him who holds the power of death - that is, the devil" (Hebrews 2:14).

"For this reason he had to be made like his brothers in every way, in order that he might become a merciful and faithful high priest in service to God, and that he might make atonement for the sins of the people" (Hebrews 2:17).

Death was in that venomous bite. Death was in that strike, but Jesus covered it by holding on to man and sacrificing Himself to see that the pain caused by our sins would be taken away.

Jacob the "*heeler*" is a picture of Jesus the "*Healer.*"

SIX

Let's Make a Deal

*"You are worthy to take the scroll and to open its seals, because
you were slain, and with your blood you purchased men for
God..."* - Revelation 5:9

Growing up I used to watch a daytime game show hosted
by Monte Hall. Contestants from the audience were chosen by
happening to have with them some obscure article called out by the
host. Once chosen, they were given a dollar figure or a more
valuable gift in exchange for their worthless item. The game
began to get interesting after they received the prize. They were
then given opportunity to risk that prize for a better one or lose it
all. Unknown prizes were waiting to be revealed behind door
number one, two, or three. The contestant needed to keep what he
had, choose a better door, or they went home with nothing. The
name of the game show of course was, *Let's Make a Deal.*

The text we'll be considering presents a similar scenario.
The question came down to, would Esau value the rights he had as
the firstborn or would he trade his birthright for what was behind
door number one, a bowl of red stew? You can almost hear the
theme music playing.

Once when Jacob was cooking some stew, Esau
came in from the open country, famished. He said
to Jacob, 'Quick, let me have some of that *red* stew!
I'm famished!' (That is why he was also called

35

Edom.) Jacob replied, 'First sell me your birthright.' 'Look, *I am about to die,*' Esau said. *'What good is the birthright to me?'* But Jacob said, 'Swear to me first.' So he swore an oath to him, selling his birthright to Jacob. Then Jacob gave Esau some *bread* and some lentil stew. He ate and drank, and then got up and left. *So Esau despised his birthright* (Genesis 25:29-34).

Let me draw your attention to the first word of this passage. It says, "once." Unfortunately, it is true that one time is all you need to lose everything you have. However, it is also true that one time is all you need to gain great success. "Once(s)" only come once. Take advantage of each one, every time. Don't despise the "once(s)" God gives you. Each one is important.

Jacob seized the opportunity. Jacob took advantage of the moment and due to the character weakness of Esau, Jacob came away on the upside of the deal of a lifetime.

In the particular moment that presented itself, all Jacob had to offer was lentil stew. Lentil stew in the scope of eternity usually isn't very much. Once you eat it, it's gone or if the stew were left too long without being eaten, it would be ruined. The soup was not lasting. It was not enduring. In other words, the soup was temporary and could only meet a momentary need.

Jacob, however, recognized he could take advantage of the moment using the momentary resources God had given him and utilize them to attain the eternal. The great missionary Jim Elliot also understood this principle. He is quoted as saying, "He is no fool who gives what he cannot keep to gain what he cannot lose."[1] If we choose, you and I can also use the momentary and temporal things we've been blessed with in life and use them for eternal

Kingdom purposes. Because Jacob understood this principle, Jacob's soup actually still tastes good today.

On the other hand there was Esau. He had a birthright blessing that would affect the rest of his life and all of eternity. The best way for me to show you what was inherent in this birthright is for me to present the nation of Israel to you. If Jacob/Israel had not purchased the birthright along with its blessings, I don't believe Israel would have been used in history as it has. Israel has been the platform for the twelve tribes, Moses, Aaron, the Law, the sacrificial system, Joshua, the Judges, David, Solomon, the prophets, and of course most importantly Jesus the Messiah and the Church. Israel, throughout history, has been supernaturally protected. Israel has and will continue to play a pivotal role in the redemptive story of our Lord. Israel remains, Edom doesn't.

Look at what God says about the younger second-born son Jacob, whose name would later be changed to Israel. God tells Moses, "say to Pharaoh, 'this is what the LORD says: *Israel is my firstborn son*, and I told you,' 'Let my son go, so he may worship me. But you refused to let him go; so I will kill your firstborn son'" (Exodus 4:22-23).

When did Israel become God's firstborn? Israel (Jacob) was actually the second-born son, but because of Jacob's great exchange with Esau, God sees Israel as the firstborn! Israel became the firstborn when he purchased the position.

All this great blessing and privilege could have been passed on to Esau and through Esau. God could have revealed Himself as the God of Abraham, Isaac and Esau. But instead, because of an insatiable appetite and a hasty decision, if you try to find Edom on a map today you won't be able to, because it no longer exists. *The second-born became the firstborn in God's sight.*

You should never base decisions on temporary circumstances for each one may have long-term consequences. You need to have God's eternal perspective in your decision-making. Don't throw away your rights with a wrong decision.

So, with no deliberation, no forethought or weighing his options, Esau jumped into a quick decision based on a temporary desire and it cost him in the long run.

I guarantee that with very little effort and certainly at a much lower price, Esau could have found something else lying around the tents to eat. After all, his father Isaac wasn't poor. We find in the next chapter of Genesis that Isaac was actually very rich. So just like Adam, who really didn't need to eat of the fruit of the tree of the knowledge of good and evil in order to become "like God" for he had already been made in the "image and likeness of God," so also Esau didn't have to sell his birthright in order to fill his stomach—but the test revealed his heart. He went for what was behind door number one and lost it all.

Do you know that mankind would not have needed the *second Adam/Jesus* if the *first Adam* had not despised all God had given him by wanting to gain more (knowledge) in his own strength (flesh/rebellion)? Have you ever imagined what it would be like if Adam had never sinned?

So, what took place with Jacob and Esau was essentially the same as what happened with Jesus and Adam. Jesus came and did what Adam should have done. Jesus came and bought what Adam didn't want. Jesus came to pay for what Adam threw away. Jesus came and reconciled that which Adam had defiled. And now, Jesus will inherit what Adam didn't merit.

38

Esau could have easily replied to Jacob, "You're joking, right? My birthright is much too valuable to even consider giving it up for something as fleeting and momentary as a single meal." But, instead of operating in faith, he was dominated by his feelings and forfeited his inheritance.

Exaggerating Esau said to Jacob, "I'm about to die." Oh, how little did he know. Oh, how little did *Esau/Adam* know he, and we, were about to die! You have to remember, what you partake of can kill you and it can and will affect others also. "For as in Adam all die, so in Christ all will be made alive" (1 Corinthians 15:22).

Next, let's look at the bargaining ability of Jacob. What a return on his investment! This servant took what was given him and instead of burying his mina (Luke 19:12-17), he received much more than a ten-fold return on his investment. He devoted the time and ingredients it took to cook some stew and he ended up with the birthright of the firstborn and all its blessings to boot. Jacob understood the importance of the firstborn rights and he desired them enough to utilize and invest what he did have to attain them. Jacob could have refused Esau the soup. Jacob could have selfishly responded like so many of us, "No, this is my soup, go get your own." Instead, like Jacob, we need to be willing to let go of the little to gain the Eternal. Esau and the rich young ruler of Matthew 19:16-24 weren't able to distinguish the difference.

This agreement was not an underhanded, heavy handed, deceptive, or manipulative move on Jacob's part. Everything was understood and done in the open. *This was a legitimate transaction of the birthright for soup.* Simply put, Esau despised and devalued the birthright, but Jacob recognized its worth and therefore purchased it. It was an oath bound, legitimate purchase of all the rights and blessings inherent in being the firstborn in *exchange* for a bowl of *red* soup.

Consider the man who owned a new Mercedes Roadster convertible, but shortly after purchasing the car he lost a large amount of money while gambling in Vegas and he found himself (famished) needing to let go of the car in order to get something less expensive. At one time he loved the car, but now he doesn't receive any pleasure from it. Instead, he begins to despise it because of the burden it's become. What if this man offered it to you far below the Fair Market Value just to take it off his hands? Would you make the deal? So would Jacob.

This is what Jesus did also. The second Adam came and made a deal, purchasing the firstborn inheritance rights that had been despised and forfeited by the first Adam. Jacob gave his *red stew*, but Jesus fulfilled the type by giving his *red blood* to purchase all the rights of the firstborn. Again, *Jacob/Jesus* purchased *Edom/Adam's* birthright with his *red stew/blood*.

Isn't it ironic the very things, the *bread/body* and *red stew/blood* from *Jacob/Jesus* that caused Esau to lose his birthright privileges in the natural are the very things we need to get our spiritual privileges back? Both Adam and Esau lost their birthright by what they ate. Jesus, on the other hand, obtained the right by what He gave, His life. Leviticus 17:11 tells us that life is in the blood.

Esau had said to Jacob, "Quick, let me have some of that red stew! I'm famished... Then *Jacob gave* Esau some bread and some lentil stew. He ate and drank, and then got up and left. *So Esau despised his birthright*" (Genesis 25:30-34).

Have you ever wondered why Matthew 18:11 reads, "For the Son of man is come to save *that* which was lost"? It doesn't say "those" who were lost. The text is referring to something different or more than people. Jesus didn't come just to save man.

40

He came to save and restore the position of man, the rights of man, and the blessings of man. The *Son of man / the second Adam / Jesus* saved *all that* was lost.

[1] Jim Elliot, 1978 hardback edition of the *Journal,* in the October 28, 1949 entry, p. 174, and 1958 hardback edition of *Shadow of the Almighty*, p. 108.

SEVEN

Deal Tales in the Details

"The first man was of the dust of the earth, the second man from heaven." - 1 Corinthians 15:47

In Genesis 27:28-29 Isaac pronounces his blessing upon Jacob. "May God give you of heaven's dew and of earth's richness — an abundance of grain and new wine. May nations serve you and peoples bow down to you. Be lord over your brothers, and may the sons of your mother bow down to you. May those who curse you be cursed and those who bless you be blessed."

These verses describe what was gained in the *birthright blessing*: heaven's dew, earth's richness, abundance, authority, respect, honor, dominion and blessing. I'm sure each of us would like to walk in these blessings, but many of us don't. From our text, we're going to learn how you can.

In Genesis 25, we saw that Jacob purchased the birthright. Two chapters later in chapter 27, we're going to see how Jacob secures all the blessings that are attached to the birthright. It is important you understand that when you get saved you get the blessings that go along with salvation also. They're *right*fully yours. The inseparable connection between the birthright and the blessings is seen in the New Covenant verses found in Hebrews 12:16-17.

43

"See that no one is sexually immoral, or is godless like Esau, who for a single meal sold his *inheritance rights* as the oldest son. Afterward, as you know, when he wanted to inherit *this blessing*, he was rejected. He could bring about no change of mind, though he sought the blessing with tears."

The blessing Esau wanted to inherit was the blessing he had the right to, until he sold it. After the sale of the birthright, the blessings then belonged to Jacob. This chapter unfolds and details elements contained within *Jesus/Jacob's* purchase.

Before we continue on to examine the appropriation of the blessings, here is a quick review of the types within our text:

Isaac - type of God
Esau - type of Adam (firstborn)(flesh)(fallen mankind)
Jacob - type of Jesus (second Adam)(the Spirit led man)
Red soup – type of red blood

At this point I want to reintroduce a thought I briefly mentioned earlier. Isaac (a type of God) is married to Rebekah. That makes them *one*. "For this reason a man will leave his father and mother and be united to his wife, and they will become one flesh" (Genesis 2:24). *The two are one.* We know that God is loving and merciful, but at the same time He is a holy and just Judge. Father God, who is the one true God, has two very different attributes. Thus, from a typological standpoint, we can see these two different characteristics of God paralleled in the union of Isaac and Rebekah. Let me show you why this is relevant.

Genesis 25:28 says, "Isaac, who had a taste for wild game, loved Esau, but Rebekah loved Jacob."

Isaac *loved* Esau/Edom. This parallels, "For God so loved the world (mankind)." God would have preferred Adam not sin. God would have preferred Adam obey Him and appreciate all the blessings He provided. God would have preferred not to send His only begotten Son, the second Adam. Still, even after *Adam/Esau/mankind* had despised his birthright, God continued to love and want *Adam/Esau/mankind* to be blessed, so He gave the firstborn blessing to the more worthy second-born Son so that through Him, He could have a *holy nation/family*. Isaac wanted a relationship with Esau just as God desires a relationship with fallen man.

Remember though, we also have Romans 9:13 which says, "Just as it is written: 'Jacob I loved, but Esau I hated.'" Here God is saying that He "hated" Esau, whom we are using as a representative of *Adam/mankind*. I want you to know that God doesn't hate man. He hates the condition of man, the sinfulness of man, the fleshliness of man due to his fallen spiritual state. We know Habakkuk 1:13 says about God, "Your eyes are too pure to look on evil; you cannot tolerate wrong." In other words, God loves because He is love and He hates sin because He is holy and just. Now, however, the object of His love (mankind) is sinful. How can this dilemma be resolved?

Enter Rebekah (remember they're one). She loved Jacob but was willing to send him "as a sacrifice" in order for him to attain the blessing. So, *Rebekah/God* came up with a plan that met the justice of God while allowing the firstborn blessings to be given to the One to whom they *right*fully belonged. That way, they would be given to One who was worthy of them. Interestingly, Rebekah means "a rope with a *noose*" and implies "captivating." It may refer to her beauty but it sounds like *justice* to me.

Let's look at how this unfolds:

45

When Isaac was old and his eyes were so weak that he could no longer see, he called for Esau his older son and said to him, 'My son.' 'Here I am,' he answered. Isaac said, 'I am now an old man and don't know the day of my death. Now then, get your weapons — your quiver and bow — and go out to the open country to hunt some wild game for me. Prepare me the kind of tasty food I like and bring it to me to eat, so that I may give you my blessing before I die' (Genesis 27:1-4).

Isaac tells *Esau/Adam/flesh/fallen mankind* that he wants to bless him, but he first has to do something. He's told to go kill some wild game and prepare it the way his father liked it.

Can you imagine what Esau was thinking when he heard all he had to do to receive the blessing was prepare a meal for his father? "I sold my birthright to Jacob, but I'm going to be able to get the blessing anyway. Jacob couldn't really have thought that our transaction was binding, could he? I'll get the blessing without Jacob even knowing. All I have to do is please the father by what I'm going to do for him."

No matter how you slice it, that's stealing. Instead of Jacob being a deceiver, perhaps deception can be found in the heart of Esau. Esau trying to take the blessing would be like me trying to get God's blessing without Jesus. I have no right to it. Jesus purchased it. It's His. I can't legally receive it unless I go through Him.

Like Esau, this is what religion does. Religion tries to get the blessing when it has no right to do so. Religion actually thinks it can be good enough or do enough to merit the blessing. The religious person proudly thinks he will receive God's blessing just because of who he is. The fact is, you and I (*Esau/mankind/the*

46

flesh) can hunt all we want but we'll never be able to bring anything to the Father the way He likes it. But *Jesus/Jacob* can and did please God exactly according to God's plan! In hindsight, the typological purpose in Isaac telling Esau he would bless him once he brought a meal was not to show Esau he could gain the blessing by what he offered, but to prove his offering wasn't going to be received by the Father at all. This is similar to the purpose of the Law. God tells us that we'll be blessed if we keep the Law, but what ends up happening is the Law teaches us that we can't keep it on our own. *Jesus/Jacob's* offering, however, was enough. The Father has received *Jesus/Jacob's* offering and is satisfied. Anything you and I try to offer would only sicken Him.

With this in mind, I want you to know that even if you could kill (crucify) your ways of *wild* living and treating life like a *game*—even if you could prepare yourself to be pleasing to the Father and begin living a perfectly sinless life, meeting the holy standards of the Father, you still were born a child of *Adam/Esau/flesh/fallen mankind.* Someone with *no rights* is a slave. The child of a slave isn't born with any more rights than his daddy. *Adam sold his rights* causing you and me to be born into slavery. Now, we need someone with a different Daddy, a holy Daddy, a heavenly Daddy to buy us back. "This is how the birth of Jesus Christ came about: His mother Mary was pledged to be married to Joseph, but before they came together, she was found to be with child through the Holy Spirit" (Matthew 1:18, 19).

Now let's examine the meal that was *not* received by the Father. Esau's offering is a type of the flesh, which never made it to the father. Oh, it makes it close, but close isn't good enough with God. Missing the mark by any amount is sin. Read Genesis 27:30-32, "After Isaac finished blessing Jacob and he had scarcely left his father's presence, his brother Esau came in from hunting. He too prepared some tasty food and brought it to his father. Then he said to him, 'My father, sit up and eat some of my game, so that you may give me your blessing.' His father Isaac asked him, '*Who are you?*'"

The question Isaac asks reminds me of God's statement on the Day of Judgment. Matthew 7:22-23 says, "Many will say to me on that day, 'Lord, Lord, did we not prophesy in your name, and in your name drive out demons and perform many miracles?' Then I will tell them plainly, '*I never knew you.* Away from me, you evildoers!'"

Who are you? I never knew you. You prepared me tasty food. You did things in my name, but my blessings are going to the One to whom they *right*ly belong. The right to the blessings has been purchased! Esau, it's too little too late!

Esau, like the scapegoat referred to in Leviticus 16, had been sent into the wilderness (open field) to get wild game. The reality for a scapegoat bearing sin was that the wild game would end up getting him, and so it is with religion. Thinking you can please the Father with something you have to offer will get you in the end. Genesis 27:2-3 says, "Now then, get your weapons—your quiver and bow—and go out to the open country to hunt some wild game for me."

Jacob, on the other hand, had different instructions to fulfill God's will. This is what Jacob was told to do:

> Now Rebekah was listening as Isaac spoke to his son Esau. When Esau left for the open country to hunt game and bring it back, Rebekah said to her son Jacob, "Look, I overheard your father say to your brother Esau, 'Bring me some game and prepare me some tasty food to eat, so that I may give you my blessing in the presence of the LORD before I die.' Now, my son, listen carefully and do

what *I* tell you: Go out to the flock and bring me *two choice young goats*, so *I* can prepare some tasty food for your father, just the way he likes it. Then take it to your father to eat, so that he may give you his blessing before he dies" (Genesis 27:5-10).

Rebekah (a type of God and specifically the justice of God) is saying, "*I will* prepare the tasty food for the Father." What we see is a type of the Justice of God preparing the sacrifice that *Jesus/Jacob* would bring. Let me explain. *Only God can please God!* "When God made his promise to Abraham, since there was no one greater for him to swear by, he swore by himself" (Hebrews 6:13-14). Only God is good. Jesus asked, "Why do you call me good?" "No one is good-except God alone." Jesus was saying that by calling Him good they were actually calling Him God, because only God is good. Only God is good enough to meet God's standards. *Rebekah/God* says, "*bring me two goats.*"

In Genesis 27:13 Rebekah said to Jacob, "My son, *let the curse fall on me.* Just do what I say; go and get them for me." This a great picture of God saying I'll pay the penalty for Justice. I'll become the perfect sacrifice. I'll put on flesh and die for the sins of the world. Let the curse fall on Me. God is making covenant with God.

Notice again, she had him get *two* goats. The symbolism continues. Leviticus 16:7-10 says,

> He shall take the *two* goats and present them before the LORD at the door of the tabernacle of meeting. Then Aaron shall cast lots for the two goats: *one lot for the LORD* and the other lot for the *scapegoat.* And Aaron shall bring the goat on which the LORD's lot fell, and offer it as a sin offering. But the goat on which the lot fell to be the scapegoat

shall be presented alive before the LORD, to make atonement upon it, and to let it go as the scapegoat into the wilderness (desert).

Here we see the Day of Atonement. This is the yearly Old Covenant method to atone for the sins of the people. To *atone* means to make amends or to make *at one*. The sacrifice to make fallen man *at one* with God was done with *two* goats. The first goat, which was chosen by the Lord's lot, would be sacrificed as a sin offering. Remember, Jacob is now the chosen firstborn (first goat to be sacrificed). The second goat (now Esau) would become the scapegoat, which would bear the sins of the people and be sent away into the wilderness. Watch what would happen:

> Then he shall *kill the goat of the sin offering*, which is for the people, bring its *blood* inside the veil, and sprinkle it on the mercy seat and before the mercy seat. So he shall make atonement for the Holy Place, because of the uncleanness of the children of Israel, and because of their transgressions, for all their sins; and so he shall do for the tabernacle of meeting which remains among them in the midst of their uncleanness (Leviticus 16:15-17).

Now let's go back to our text in Genesis. Here we have Rebekah telling Jacob to get *two* goats. The *Esau/Adam/Fallen man/scapegoat bearing sins* represents God's judgment by being sent into the open field and returning to the Father's question, "*who are you?*" Then, we have the picture of the second born *Jesus/Jacob* goat that is obedient to the Justice of *Rebekah/God* presenting himself to the Father as the firstborn, while actually wearing the skin of a sacrificed goat. The Father accepts this meal. To help solidify this type of *Jesus/Jacob* being the atoning sacrifice, look at what else Jacob brought to the Father:

50

Genesis 27:17 says, "Then she handed to her son Jacob the tasty food and the *bread* she had made." And what else?

Genesis 27:25-26 says that, "Jacob brought it to him and he ate; and he brought some *wine* and he drank. Then his father Isaac said to him, "Come here, my son, and kiss me.""

The Genesis account sounds a lot like Matthew 26:26-28. "Jesus took bread, gave thanks and broke it, and gave it to his disciples, saying, 'Take and eat; this is my body.' Then he took the cup, gave thanks and offered it to them, saying, 'Drink from it, all of you. This is my blood of the covenant, which is poured out for many for the forgiveness of sins.'"

Jacob brought his father a sacrificial goat, and it's also recorded that he brought him *bread and wine*. This too is what Jesus did. Jesus brought the bread and wine (His body and blood) and presented Himself to the Father as a sacrificial lamb *(using the Passover type)* or goat *(using the Atonement type)*. The Father partook of the meal and was pleased.

Do you know that Jesus' offering would have been meaningless for us if the Father hadn't received it? I have good news though. The Father received what *Jesus/Jacob* had to offer, and if we come to the Father in Jesus, He'll receive us too. "For Christ did not enter a man-made sanctuary that was only a copy of the true one; *he entered heaven itself, now to appear for us in God's presence*" (Hebrews 9:24). "How much more, then, will the *blood of Christ*, who through the eternal Spirit *offered himself unblemished to God*, cleanse our consciences from acts that lead to death, so that we may serve the living God! For this reason *Christ is the mediator*" (Hebrews 9:14-15).

Rebekah/God prepared the offering just like *Isaac/God* liked it. Then *Jesus/Jacob/God* obediently presented himself *with/as* the sacrifice. This is how it went in the Genesis account:

> So he went and got them and brought them to his mother, and she prepared some tasty food, just the way his father liked it. Then Rebekah took the *best clothes of Esau* her older son, which she had in the house, and *put them on her younger son Jacob.* She also *covered* his hands and the smooth part of his neck *with the goatskins.* Then she handed to her son Jacob the tasty food and the bread she had made (Genesis 27:14-17).

The younger son Jacob put on the older firstborn son's clothes. Remember, if Esau had not sold his birthright, the blessing would have normally gone to him because he was the firstborn. The blessing goes to the firstborn. So, in order to get the firstborn blessing, *the second-born Jesus/Jacob had to come as the firstborn.* Jesus could not have received the blessing by coming as an animal. He could not have received it by coming as an angel. He could not even have received it by coming as *Himself/God. God had to become a man in order to redeem man. Jesus (Jehovah is salvation) / Jacob (heel grasper)* came as *Adam / Edom (red).* This is what He did:

"The Word became flesh and made his dwelling among us" (John 1:14).

"So it is written: 'The first man Adam became a living being'; the last Adam, a life-giving spirit. The spiritual did not come first, but the natural, and after that the spiritual. The *first man* was of the dust of the earth, the *second man* from heaven" (1 Corinthians 15:45-48).

1 John 4:2 says, "Every spirit that acknowledges that *Jesus Christ has come in the flesh* is from God."

John 10:1-4 says,

> I tell you the truth, the man who does not enter the sheep pen by the *gate*, but climbs in by some other way, is a thief and a robber. The man who enters by the *gate* is the shepherd of his sheep. The watchman opens the gate for him, and the sheep listen to his voice. He calls his own sheep by name and leads them out. When he has brought out all his own, he goes on ahead of them, and his sheep follow him because they know his voice. (One interpretation of *gate* is natural birth).

Now, when *Jesus/Jacob* put on the best of Esau's clothes (flesh), he also put on the goatskins. So, not only did *Jesus/Jacob* come looking like the firstborn, he also came looking like a lamb/goat. He became the sacrificial *Man/Lamb* who would cover the sins of *Adam/Esau/fallen man.* John 1:29 says, "The next day John saw Jesus coming toward him and said, 'Look, the Lamb of God, who takes away the sin of the world!'" The Lamb of God then became a goat so we "goats" could become sheep (Matthew 25:32-33). I don't want the picture to become too abstract, but let me explain one more thing regarding Jesus fulfilling the Day of Atonement. At the cross Jesus actually was the fulfillment of both goats. The cross was where He took the sins of fallen man upon Himself, although He had none of His own. He bore the judgment of the Esau goat outside the city. As the Esau goat He cried, "My God, my God, why have you forsaken me" (Matthew 27:46)? As the Jacob goat He called in a loud voice, "Father, into your hands I commit my spirit." When he had said this, he breathed his last (Luke 23:46). Jesus was the cleansing goat whose blood was placed upon the Mercy Seat, but He also bore our judgment as a sin bearing scapegoat.

Now, take a look back at Genesis to see what Jacob had to say. Genesis 27:18-19 tells us, "He went to his father and said, 'My father.' 'Yes, my son,' he answered. 'Who is it?' Jacob said to his father, 'I am Esau your firstborn. I have done as you told me. Please sit up and eat some of my game so that you may give me your blessing.'"

I know, in context, Jacob was lying when he said, "I am Esau (hairy)," but because he was wearing the goatskins he, in fact, was hairy (Esau). And, then he said, "I have done as 'you' told me." Jacob had actually been told by Rebekah. But remember, typologically if you consider Rebekah and Isaac as one, then Isaac did tell him. So, typologically out of love for *Esau/fallen man* He (*Isaac/God*) told one goat to go to the open field and for the sake of God's justice, He (*Rebekah/God*) told the other goat to put on the firstborn's clothes, wear "hairy" goatskins, and present the bread and wine to the Father.

We see then, that Jacob was simply being obedient, just as Jesus was obedient. We know that Christ learned obedience by what he suffered (Hebrews 5:8) and that He humbled himself and became obedient to death - even death on a cross (Philippians 2:8).

Again, the second-born *Jesus/Jacob* came as an obedient sinless firstborn *Adam/Esau*. Jesus, the second Adam, came as a sinless first Adam to get the blessing the first Adam forfeited by despising what he had.

Genesis 27:20-24 goes on to say,

Isaac asked his son, 'How did you find it so quickly, my son?' 'The LORD your God gave me success,' he replied. Then Isaac said to Jacob, 'Come near so I can touch you, my son, to know whether you really are my son Esau or not.' Jacob went close to his father Isaac, who touched him and said, '*The voice is the voice of Jacob, but the hands are the hands of Esau.*' He did not recognize him, for his hands were hairy like those of his brother Esau; so he blessed him. 'Are you really my son Esau?' he asked. '*I am,*' he replied.

There is so much contained within these four verses, but I'm going to briefly mention only a few points. First, Jacob was quick to obey. Jesus was also quick to obey and we should be too. When you're quick to obey, God can quickly give you success. Then, when it's asked of you, "Why are you so blessed?" you can respond like Jacob, "God gave me success."

Next, let me point out that the Father says, "Come near so I can touch you, my son." This is significant because sinful man cannot come into the presence of the Father. Man, because of his sin, has been alienated and sent off into the wilderness. Even if we were to try coming close to the Father He would ask, "Who are you?" He wouldn't recognize us. But, praise God we have an elder brother who has been received by the Father. Our older brother has been blessed by the Father and now enables us to come near through Him.

Then we read that Isaac recognizes the voice to be that of Jacob, but the hands were the hands of Esau. Let me say it this way. The word he was hearing was as if it were the Word of *Jesus/Jacob/God*, but the hands were the hands of a man (Esau). Yes, praise God, the Word became flesh! Isaac was indeed hearing the Word of *Jesus/Jacob*, but when he touched his hands it was as if he were touching the hands of his natural firstborn, a man (Adam).

Life and/or death are in the power of the tongue (Proverbs 18:21). We can speak with the voice of *Jesus/Jacob/Spirit* and bring life, or speak with the voice of *Esau/Adam/Flesh* and bring death. Speak words of life. At the same time we speak life-affirming words, however, we also need to have flesh and blood hands that can touch and hold and relate and reach out to a hurting world. We are the hands and feet of Jesus on the earth today.

Finally, notice how Jacob replies to his father when asked if he really were Esau. His response was *"I am."* This is reminiscent of God revealing to Moses, "I Am that I Am" and Jesus saying in John 8:58, "before Abraham was born, I am!" Yes, Jesus is man, but He is also God. Yes, Jesus put on *Esau/flesh*, but He always remained the Great *I Am!*

So again, what we have recorded here is a beautiful picture of the great exchange; God becoming like us so we can become like Him. Or, in other words, "The second-born became the firstborn in order to become the firstborn of all who would be born again." Amen!

Now, before we move on to some new material let me bring you back to verse one of chapter 27. It says of *Isaac/God* that, "his eyes were so weak that *he could no longer see.*" I have to ask, what is the one thing God can no longer see? That's right, your sin and mine if we're in Christ Jesus (the firstborn). Our sin is now as far away as the East is from the West. It has been thrown into the sea of forgetfulness. The penalty has been paid, and Jesus has taken away the sins of the world.

"I, even I, am he who blots out your transgressions, for my own sake, and remembers your sins no more" (Isaiah 43:25).

God doesn't see how the firstborn despised his birthright. He doesn't know the firstborn failed, missed the mark and sinned.

When I come to the Father in Jesus, I come *justified; just-if-I'd* never sinned. When the second-born came, He came as a *sinless firstborn* Adam (man), just as if the firstborn had never sinned or despised his birthright. Jesus looked like the firstborn, smelled like the firstborn, felt like the firstborn, did what the firstborn was supposed to do, responded as the firstborn should have responded, and in every respect purchased the rights of the firstborn and was then justifiably the recipient of the *blessings of the firstborn*. And, let me give you a prelude of what's to come. He then becomes the firstborn of a nation of born-again sons and daughters. He becomes the firstborn of many brethren!

Truly Jesus is the fulfillment of the type seen in the meal Jacob presented to his father. Jesus is also the fulfillment of the Day of Atonement. Indeed, Jesus is the substitute for *Adam/Edom/man*. As our substitute, *Jesus/Jacob* has redeemed the position of authority, respect, honor, and dominion that *Esau/Adam* had lost. *Jesus/Jacob* has also redeemed the abundance of heaven's dew, the earth's richness, and all of the Father's blessings that *Esau/Adam* had forfeited.

The blessing has been bestowed back to man through the man, Jesus.

57

EIGHT

Deal Me In

"If anyone is in Christ, he is a new creation; the old has gone, the new has come!" - 2 Corinthians 5:17

You may have heard that if you want to join a card game, all you have to say is, "deal me in." Everything we've studied to this point has been in reference to what Jacob has attained. *Jesus/Jacob* has received everything the Father had to give. Jacob was dealt what looked like a losing hand, but he ended up with a royal flush. That's great for *Jesus/Jacob*, but how do we get in on this deal? If Jesus has possession of it all, is there anything left for us? And if there is, what must we do to receive it? Is there anything we're to kill and prepare that will please the Father today?

According to Romans 12, we're told to offer our bodies as living sacrifices. But, what does this mean? We know that if we want to be blessed we can't come on our own merits, or in our own righteousness. We know we can't come representing ourselves because we aren't the firstborn. Even if we were, like Adam and Esau, we don't have what it takes to live up to the character qualifications and standards the Father requires. We don't look like we should. We don't sound like we should. We don't feel like we should. We don't even smell like we should. Ultimately, even though *Esau/Adam* would like to have pleased the Father, what he had to offer never even reached Him. It's the same with us—even if we want to please God, what we have to offer falls far too short.

Romans 3:23-25 says, "All have sinned and fall short of the glory of God, and are justified freely by his grace through the redemption that came by Christ Jesus. God presented him as a sacrifice of atonement, through faith in his blood."

We can't offer what He offered. His offering was perfect. He brought food prepared just the way the Father liked it. Jesus brought the food of obedience. Jesus said, "My food is to do the will of the one who sent me." Obedience is always better than sacrifice. Obedience may require sacrifice, but sacrifice without obedience will not be accepted. And sacrifice on our own terms isn't sacrifice. Blessings are only appropriated when we come according to His protocol.

In this section, we'll briefly break down how the great exchange secured by *Jesus/Jacob,* applies to you and me.

The living sacrifice that we are to present is a life that is *dead to the flesh,* but *alive to the things of the Spirit by faith in the firstborn Jesus.*

The living sacrifice that we are to offer is also described in Romans 8:10 where it tells us, "But if Christ is in you, your body is dead because of sin, yet your spirit is alive because of righteousness."

Similarly Galatians 2:20 says, "I have been crucified with Christ and I no longer live, but Christ lives in me. The life I live in the body, I live by *faith in* the Son of God, who loved me and gave himself for me."

Let me elaborate in light of our study. The picture is repeating itself. This is what God did in Jesus and now wants to duplicate in you. God wants to get *Jesus/Jacob* in your *Esau/flesh*. Again, if Christ is *in you*, then your flesh is considered dead because of the sin that has been laid upon it. Yet, your spirit is alive because the One who offered the acceptable atoning sacrifice for you is in you. Let me say it this way: Jesus *in* your sk*in* takes away your s*in* and makes you k*in*. We need Jesus in our life! We need Him in our heart. But, not only does He need to be in us, we also need to be in Him. "If a man remains in me *and* I in him, he will bear much fruit; apart from me you can do nothing" (John 15:5).

When going to the Father, we must do so *by faith*. Remember, "Without faith it is impossible to please God" (Hebrews 11:6). But the faith we go by is faith that we are *in* Jesus. It is not faith that there is a God. It is not faith that you can go to God. It is not faith that the Father will accept you. It is faith that the only reason you can go to the Father and that He'll accept you is because you are *in* Christ.

If you want to be blessed, you have to come wearing Him, under His covering, the covering of the firstborn. He covered Himself with the best of Esau's garments (flesh) so we could be covered in His righteousness. "Blessed are they whose transgressions are forgiven, whose *sins are covered*. Blessed is the man whose sin the Lord will never count against him" (Romans 4:7-8).

When you know you're in Christ and Christ is in you, you can say along with Isaiah, "I delight greatly in the LORD; my soul rejoices in my God. For he has clothed me with garments of salvation and arrayed me in a robe of righteousness" (Isaiah 61:10).

Once you are *in* Christ Jesus *by faith*, you too can say of yourself that you are a *joint-heir with Jesus*. Romans 8:16-17 says, "The Spirit itself beareth witness with our spirit, that we are the children of God: And if children, then heirs; heirs of God, and joint-heirs with Christ" (KJV). Everything Jesus has been given also becomes ours by virtue of our position in Him.

His success, *when harnessed by faith*, is your success. "The LORD your God gave me success, he (Jacob) replied" (Genesis 27:20 parenthesis mine). When you know *Jesus/Jacob*, you know the one who knows how to get the best out of life. He knows how to get that which is lasting and eternal. He knows how to acquire treasures moth and rust does not corrupt. He has secured God's success. Now, if you want to be successful, you need to go through Him.

His relationship with the Father, *when accessed by faith*, can be your relationship with the Father. "But now in Christ Jesus you who once were far away have been brought near through the blood of Christ" (Ephesians 2:13).

For example, every time I go to the Father in the name of Jesus, even though I have imperfections, areas of compromise, and don't say everything perfectly, if I am in Jesus the Father won't see (recognize) the carnal me. The Father may say something like, "the voice sounds like Gary, but the hands are the hands of Jesus and this offering sure pleases Me." In the last chapter we saw how Jesus came in *flesh/Adam*, now if we want to get in on the deal, we must come in Him. *Jesus/Jacob* has to be our covering.

"Jacob went close to his father Isaac, who touched him and said, 'The voice is the voice of Jacob, but the hands are the hands of Esau.' *He did not recognize him*, for his hands were hairy like those of his brother Esau" (Genesis 27:22, 23).

Once again, the Father might say, "The voice sounds like Frank, Joe, or Sue but I can't see the sin. It sounds like Helen, but they're coming in the name of Jesus and I know it's my Son because I feel the nail scars in his hands. He/she has the hands of my only begotten firstborn Son." When we are in Jesus, the Father doesn't see our sin. He sees His sinless Son.

So then, you don't need to be afraid the Father will recognize you for who you are and curse you. You don't need to feel guilty. Remember, Jesus let the curse fall upon Himself. Deuteronomy 21:23 says, "Anyone who is hung on a tree is under God's curse." You don't need to think; "I can't go to the Father because He's going to see me for the dirty no-good scoundrel that I am." That line of thinking is correct if you go on your own, but if you go in the firstborn, then He only sees the firstborn. If you go in the firstborn, you'll get the same results as the firstborn. And, when you go to the Father in Christ, you do not need to think it may *appear* as *trickery* or *deception*. You do not need to feel guilty going to the Father in the name of Jesus. What were the results of *Jesus/Jacob* going to the Father as the firstborn? The Father blessed Him! Now, if you go *in* Him and *in* His name, you too will be blessed!

NINE

Flesh Out

"Flesh gives birth to flesh, but the Spirit gives birth to spirit."
- John 3:6

Have you ever seen someone erupt in anger, act like a spoiled brat, or just simply give into sinful indulgences? You might refer to the actions of that person as "fleshing out." People who do these things are obviously acting in the flesh with no concern for the Spirit or other people. *Esau/flesh* ended up being the one sent out to the wilderness and ultimately was not accepted by the Father. "Jacob I loved but *Esau I hated.*"

Our study will now begin to pick up pace with regards to the amount of Scriptural text we cover. The exchange has taken place. *Jesus/Jacob* bought the birthright. The father granted the blessing. *Esau/flesh* returned from hunting and the father asked, "Who are you?"

The type begins to breaks down a little at this point because Isaac started to tremble at his "mistake." Of course with God, there is no slipping anything past Him. Isaac then asked, "Who was it then that gave me something to eat?" "He's the one I blessed and indeed he will be blessed."

Isaac also tells Esau in chapter 27:35, "Thy brother came with subtilty, and hath taken away thy blessing" (KJV). Subtilty can also be translated deceitfully, but for the purposes of this study, I will use the King James interpretation. Subtilty carries the connotation of being sly by skill or ingenuity without necessarily lying.

Esau/flesh then replies to his father in verse 36, "Isn't he rightly named Jacob? He has deceived me these two times: He took my birthright, and now he's taken my blessing!" That's how the New International Version translation reads. Now let me show you a translation that reads closer to the original Hebrew from Young's Literal Translation. "Is it because [one] called his name Jacob that he doth *take me by the heel* these two times? My birthright he hath taken; and lo, now, he hath taken my blessing."

Hold on. Let's add this up. There are actually three times, not two, that Scripture records Jacob grabbing the heel of Esau: #1 at birth, #2 upon purchasing the birthright, and #3 upon receiving the blessing. We know Jesus came to give us life and life more abundantly, right? Not only do we get the *new birth*, we also get the *rights* and the abundant life *blessings* that go with being a new creature in Christ Jesus. Note that in each of these cases Jacob in no way deceives Esau. He could not have been deceptive as a newborn. He purchased the birthright openly and legally. And lastly, any question of deception in regards to obtaining the blessing was between he and his father, not Esau.

Jacob definitely *grabbed Esau's heel*, and Esau may not have understood what happened, but Jacob certainly never *deceived* him.

As the bitter dialog between the Father and *Esau/flesh* continues, Isaac at no time corrects what has been done. Isaac doesn't curse or rebuke Jacob and then pronounce the blessing upon *Esau/flesh*. No, the blessing went to whom it *right*ly belonged. Not only does Isaac never speak negatively of Jacob, but also even more importantly, nowhere in Scripture does God condemn the actions of Jacob. What Isaac ends up doing is telling Esau in verse 37, "I have made him lord over you and have made all his relatives his servants, and I have sustained him with grain and new wine. So what can I possibly do for you, my son?"

In this verse the Father is telling the *flesh* that *Jesus/Jacob* has been made Lord. Yes, it is true, *Jesus is Lord over all flesh and everything and everyone that relates to Him must serve Him.* His name is above every name and every knee will bow and every tongue confess that Jesus Christ is Lord! The Father has given Him grain (which is the substance of bread, and bread is a type of the Word) and He has given Him the new wine (the Holy Spirit) to sustain Him.

Luke 4:1-2 says, "Jesus, *full of the Holy Spirit*, returned from the Jordan and was *led by the Spirit* in the desert, where for forty days he was tempted by the devil." We all know that Jesus resisted every temptation of the devil with the Word (bread). Both the Word and the Spirit did sustain Him. Not only did they sustain Jesus, but they will sustain you and me also.

So, what is left for the Father to do for *Esau/flesh*? Absolutely nothing. All blessing, glory and honor have gone to Jesus! In turn, we have been given all things that pertain to life and godliness through Christ (2 Peter 1:3). It is in Him we live, move and have our being (Acts 17:28)!

Upon hearing this terrible news from Isaac, Genesis 27:38 says, "Then Esau wept aloud." This reminds me of Matthew 25:29-30 where it says, "For everyone who has will be given more, and he will have an abundance. Whoever does not have, even what he has will be taken from him. And throw that worthless servant outside, into the darkness, where there will be *weeping* and gnashing of teeth."

The Father then goes on to tell the *flesh,* "Your dwelling will be away from the earth's richness, away from the dew of heaven above. You will live by the sword and you will serve your brother. But when you grow restless, you will throw his yoke from off your neck" (Genesis 27:39-40).

Flesh, as it says in Galatians, will reap corruption in both this life and the life to come. The flesh keeps you from earthly and heavenly treasures. In its quest to gain these treasures and to attain "the blessing," the flesh has to resort to the sword. The flesh has to live by the sword to make things happen. The flesh uses might and power. God, on the other hand says, "Not by might nor by power but by my Spirit" (Zechariah 4:6).

There is some good news for the flesh though; you will serve your brother! You may not think its good news and you may not even realize when you're serving Him, but you will serve the Spirit. You will serve Jesus. God is sovereign and He will even use your rebellion for His purposes. God will use the restlessness of Pharaoh, king Nebuchadnezzar, and Judas to bring about His will. Unfortunately for the flesh, when it grows restless (because it wants things now, and it wants things it's way) it rebels and throws off His yoke, even though His yoke is easy and His burden is light. The flesh just can't rest in what He's done. The flesh has to do everything for itself.

Romans 7:22-25 says,

> For I delight in the Law of God in my inmost self [with my new nature]. But I discern in my bodily members [in the sensitive appetites and wills of the flesh] a different law (rule of action) at war against the law of my mind (my reason) and making me a prisoner to the law of sin that dwells in my bodily organs [in the sensitive appetites and wills of the

flesh]. O unhappy and pitiable and wretched man that I am! Who will release and deliver me from [the shackles of] this body of death? O thank God! [He will!] through Jesus Christ (the Anointed One) our Lord! (Amplified Version)

Jacob has delivered us from the rule of Esau! What a mess it would have been if Isaac had given all the rights and blessings to Esau. What a mess if Adam had been allowed to eat from the Tree of Life after the Fall. It would have been a super-sized prodigal son experience! Praise God, *Jesus/Jacob* received it all instead.

Now, let's look at some common characteristics of the flesh. This will help in ridding you of the flesh before you "flesh out."

First, I want you to see that the flesh may genuinely want to be blessed by the Father. "When Esau heard his father's words, he burst out with a loud and bitter cry and said to his father, 'Bless me — me too, my father!' Then he asked, 'Haven't you reserved any blessing for me'" (Genesis 27:34, 36)?

Esau certainly wanted the blessing. Flesh always likes to feel good and be blessed. The flesh always likes immediate gratification and is always concerned about how it feels. Do you know anyone like this? Unfortunately, there are no blessings reserved for those who try to please God or themselves in the flesh. The only way to please the Father and to live a satisfied and fulfilled life is to do so by the Spirit. The only way to reap true life is to sow to the Spirit. Galatians 6:8-9 tells us, "For he who sows to his flesh will of the flesh reap corruption, but he who sows to the Spirit will of the Spirit reap everlasting life."

Second, Flesh always thinks it deserves. Those with a carnal mindset think they have it coming to them. They think they've earned it, and that they have the (birth) right. They think it's not fair when they are not treated the way they "deserve." The truth is, however, if we received what we deserved then we'd all have hell to pay. Everything we receive above hell is God's grace.

Third, *Esau/flesh* holds a grudge. "Esau *held a grudge* against Jacob because of the blessing his father had given him. *He said to himself,* 'the days of mourning for my father are near; then *I will kill* my brother Jacob'" (Genesis 27:41).

Keep in mind, flesh always wants its way and one area in which this is true is in regards to justice. Flesh cannot give God the vengeance that belongs to Him. If a person is demanding justice on his own terms, it's not God.

Esau held this grudge because of the blessings Jacob received. The flesh hates to see anyone else succeed. This is something you must understand—not everyone will be happy for you when good things come your way. Not everyone wants to see you prosper. Flesh compares flesh with flesh.

The flesh lives by the sword and is willing to kill anything that stands in its way. Esau planned to kill Jacob. The flesh and Spirit are diametrically opposed and because of this the flesh will try to snuff out the Spirit at any chance it gets. Remember, the flesh (men) wanted to kill Jesus also. "He came to that which was his own, but his own did not receive him. Yet to all who received him, to those who believed in his name, he gave the *right* to become children of God - children born not of natural descent, nor of human decision or a husband's will, but born of God" (John 1:11-13).

"When Rebekah *was told* what Esau her older son had said, she sent for her younger son Jacob and said to him, "Your brother

70

Esau is consoling himself with the thought of killing you" (Genesis 27:42).

Notice that Esau hadn't told anyone about his plans. The text says, *"he said to himself"* (v. 41) that he was going to kill Jacob. In order to protect Jacob, it appears God revealed the intent of Esau's heart to Rebekah. For only God knows the thoughts and intentions of a man. Rebekah, in turn, told Jacob to flee to her brother Laban in Haran until Esau's anger subsided. At which point, she said, "I'll send word for you to come back from there" (Genesis 27:45). Interestingly, Scripture does not record Rebekah (our type of God and specifically the Justice of God) calling Jacob back, but instead it is God Himself who gives word for Jacob to return home.

The fourth characteristic of flesh is that it is attracted to its own kind. Flesh attracts flesh. The text goes on to say in verse 46, how disgusted Rebekah was with Esau's Hittite wives. If you go back to Genesis 26:34-35, it tells us that these wives were a source of grief to Isaac and Rebekah. Esau had chosen to marry into that which was revolting to the Lord.

Flesh, no matter how hard it tries to the contrary, will hook up and unite with flesh. On the other hand, the Word tells us in 2 Corinthians 6:14-16,

Do not be yoked together with unbelievers. For what do righteousness and wickedness have in common? Or what fellowship can light have with darkness? What harmony is there between Christ and Belial? What does a believer have in common with an unbeliever? What agreement is there between the temple of God and idols? For we are the temple of the living God.

The Word of God also tells us in 1 Corinthians 15:33-34, "Do not be misled: 'Bad company corrupts good character.' Come back to your senses as you ought, and stop sinning."

Some of the things Christians come into agreement with, laugh at, and even do when they get together with friends ought to grieve their spirit. What you are attracted to and whom you associate with displays what is in you. I can tell where you are at spiritually by whom you spend your time with. All I have to do is sit back and watch, and the fruit reveals how the tree is doing.

Now remember, Rebekah told Jacob to flee from Esau. Likewise, sometimes the Spirit simply needs to flee. After numerous warnings in the book of Ezekiel, the Holy Spirit left the Temple. After his sin with Bathsheba David prayed, "Do not cast me from your presence or *take your Holy Spirit from me*" (Psalm 51:11). When the flesh repeatedly rejects the Spirit, you have to stop casting your pearls before the swine, wipe the dust off your feet, and go somewhere else. When you continually offer Jacob and they persistently choose Esau, there's a time to "deliver such a one unto Satan for the destruction of the flesh (Esau), that the spirit may be saved in the day of the Lord Jesus" (1 Corinthians 5:5).

Before his flight to Laban, Isaac confirms the blessing upon Jacob and tells him not to marry a Canaanite woman. When Esau heard his father's command for Jacob to not marry a Canaanite woman, he finally realized how displeasing his wives were to his father. In an attempt to get back into his father's graces, he decided he was going to marry into Abraham's family. Look at what he does—"Esau then realized how displeasing the Canaanite women were to his father Isaac; so *he went to Ishmael and married Mahalath*, the sister of Nebaioth and daughter of Ishmael son of Abraham, *in addition* to the wives he already had" (Genesis 28:8-9).

Note that Esau did not disown his current wives. He did not repent and send his foreign wives away as Ezra would have the exiles do hundreds of years later. Instead he took an additional wife from the family. Yes, he took a wife who was in fact a descendant from Abraham, but look at what side of the family he takes her from. He took her from the family of flesh, Ishmael. Do you remember how Abraham took things into his own hands trying to make the Word of God come to pass through Hagar?

Instead of Esau marrying into the promise, he marries into Ishmael. He marries into the flesh. Again, flesh is always fleshly even when it's trying to please the Father. And, anything outside of the promise is flesh. Anything outside of *Jesus/Jacob* will not please the Father.

The woman Esau marries is named Mahalath. Mahalath means, "sickness." Why would he want to marry into something weak, anemic, and sick? I'm sure that was not his intent. No one wants sickness, death, and separation from God, but when it's a flesh response there can be no other result. So, although Esau took a wife who was not "of the daughters of Canaan," neither did he marry into the family of promise. Therefore, he remained outside the promise.

If you and I want God's blessings in our lives, then we need to go about getting them God's way. We have to crucify the flesh and go through *Jesus/Jacob*. *Jacob I loved, but Esau I hated.*

TEN

Rock of Revelation

"…and on this rock I will build my church, and the gates of Hades will not overcome it." - Matthew 16:17-19

Isaac's blessing upon Jacob is basically the same promise God had given to Abraham. It would be through Jacob that the promise is fulfilled. Jacob is the child of promise. Jacob flees from *Esau/flesh* and sets out to live under *Laban/Law*. On his journey a beautiful picture of the Bride of Christ begins to develop.

Before we delve into the details, take a look at the big picture: Jacob sets out for Beersheba with both birthright and blessing to find a bride from his own family. Securing the birthright and blessings has been accomplished, but before he can be intimate and produce offspring with his bride, Laban has to be dealt with. Just as Jacob worked for Laban, in order to get himself a bride, so Jesus fulfilled the Law to get the church. Laban then is a type of the Law while the bride, of course, is a type of the church. On his way to this objective, Jacob stops for the night and has an encounter with God. Let's take a look at this experience to see if we might recognize anything familiar.

When he reached a *certain place*, he stopped for the night because the sun had set. Taking one of the stones there, *he put it under his head* and *lay down to sleep.* He had a dream in which he saw a *stairway resting on the earth, with its top reaching to heaven, and the angels of God were ascending and descending on it.* There above it stood the LORD, and he said: 'I am the LORD, the God of your father Abraham and the God of Isaac. I will give you and your descendants the land on which you are lying. Your descendants will be like the dust of the earth, and you will spread out to the west and to the east, to the north and to the south. All peoples on earth will be blessed through you and your offspring. I am with you and will watch over you wherever you go, and *I will bring you back to this land.* I will not leave you until I have done what I have promised you' (Genesis 28:11-15).

First, notice what is revealed in the dream. God confirms to *Jesus/Jacob* that the blessing Isaac just declared in chapter 28 as well as the promise Abraham received in Genesis 17 each apply to him.

As with Jacob, God requires each of us to work at making someone else's dream, vision, or promise come to pass. In doing so, you will see your own come to fruition. For example: when you or I respond to the Great Commission, we're responding to a command given to someone else before we received it. The Commission was originally given to the twelve apostles. They passed that Word on to others who in turn passed it on. So in reality, we're actually helping to fulfill a Commission that was given to Jesus' first followers.

When we function the way God designed, we will always be carrying out someone else's vision. David had to serve Saul. Solomon built his father's dream. Elisha had to serve and follow Elijah before receiving a double portion. You and I have to find a place to serve to see our own promises fulfilled. I am serving under my pastor. I am carrying out his vision, while at the same time I'm stepping into my own. There are no separate, do it alone, apart from the body, ministries. If you're doing it alone with no covering, it's not God. Remember, we're the body of Christ and He is the head. The vision of Abraham, Isaac and Jacob must become your vision.

Jacob could have said, "That was grandpa's promise. I want something else; something that's my own; something different than dad and grandpa had. I want something more exciting." But, when God speaks a Word, it's an ever-expanding Word. "Let there be light," is still affecting you and me today! This promise to Jacob, all the way down to, "*I will bring you back to this land* (typologically the Second Coming)," will be completed in and through Christ.

So, our text begins by telling us, "When he reached a *certain place*, he stopped for the night because the sun had set. Taking one of the *stones* there, he put it *under his head* and lay down to sleep" (Genesis 28:11). I believe God wants each of us to come to a point in our walk with Him where we reach a *certain* place. I know this is referring to a particular, specific locality that Jacob had arrived at but I also believe God wants us to reach a place within ourselves that we are *certain* about who Jesus is and what He expects of our lives. Jacob, in our text, reaches a certain place, and I know Jesus was always certain about what He said, where He was going, and the relationship He had with the Father. Like Jacob, in order for you and me to be *certain* every move we make is *certain*ly the Father's will; we have to receive a revelation. The *certain* place Jacob was able to rest in was a place of revelation and confirmation that God was leading him.

Receiving revelation is part of the *Jesus/Jacob* experience. Notice, Esau isn't the one who receives these revelations. Esau isn't having a spiritual dream. God deals with Spirit people. He doesn't communicate His plans or direct the ungodly and flesh-ruled person. But, the sons of God are led by the Spirit of God (Romans 8:14). The children of God play a role in the building and advancement of His kingdom. We are part of what He is building.

So my question is, "Does God speak to you? Can you hear His voice?" John 10:4-5 says, "He goes on ahead of them, and his sheep follow him because they know his voice. But they will never follow a stranger." My prayer for you is that you come to a place of immovable, unshakable faith in the Lord. I pray your relationship with Him becomes so close that you have a certainty that every step, I mean every step, is ordered of the Lord. "The steps of a good man are ordered by the LORD" (Psalm 37:23 KJV). I pray that you will come to know that God orders your steps not based on your own goodness, but because of the righteousness you have in the firstborn. So, when you are in Christ, you are righteous and because you are righteous in Him, He orders your steps.

Let's return to the picture. The text goes on to tell us that when *Jesus/Jacob* arrived at this certain place he took a *stone* and placed it *under his head* to sleep on (Genesis 28:11). This was common practice in Jacob's day. Travelers didn't carry a fluffy pillow along with them. Instead, they would find a rock that was near their campsite to sleep on.

Many times in Scripture, a rock is likened to a revelation. While resting on this particular rock, Jacob has a revelation of God, and when he awakes he calls that place the house of God. The house of God, of course, is a picture of the church. This whole revelatory experience happening to Jacob can be compared to Peter's New Testament revelation of Jesus being the Christ. Upon Peter's revelation Jesus replied, "Blessed are you, Simon son of Jonah, for this was not revealed to you by man, but by my Father in heaven. And I tell you that you are Peter, and *on this rock I will build my church*, and the gates of Hades will not overcome it" (Matthew 16:17-19).

In another place Jesus said, "Therefore everyone who *hears these words of mine* and puts them into practice is like a wise man who built his house on the *rock*" (Matthew 7:24-27).

The church is based on a revelation and that revelation is a rock. Notice that the rock (of revelation) is placed under Jacob's head. It is upon the rock of revelation and under the *head*ship of *Jesus/Jacob* that the church is built. Colossians 1:18 says, "And *he is the head* of the body, *the church*; he is the beginning and the firstborn from among the dead, so that in everything he might have the supremacy."

The Genesis account continues,

When Jacob awoke from his sleep, he thought, "Surely the LORD is in this place, and I was not aware of it." He was afraid and said, "How awesome is this place! This is none other than the house of God; this is the gate of heaven" (Genesis 28:16-17).

Here Jacob declares this place of revelation to be an "awesome place" and says, "This is none other than the house of God; this is the gate of heaven." Do you see it? When a person receives the revelation that Jesus is the Christ that person becomes the church. That person becomes the temple of the Holy Ghost (I Corinthians 6:19). God makes your place His place. Knowing that the Lord has taken His place in your place is an awesome place to be in.

Ultimately, Jacob's account can be viewed in reference to Jesus because we know thousands of years later Jesus also rested, went to sleep (died), and laid his head down in a tomb hewn of stone in order to fulfill the dream that messengers could ascend and descend between heaven and earth. Jesus restored communication and access between God and man. Jesus, like Jacob, could then say, "How awesome is this place! This is none other than the house of God" (Genesis 28:17). This is why He went to sleep (died), and this is why He woke up (rose from the dead) early Sunday morning – to get a church!

The place of revelation is the house of God of which I am a living stone under His *head*ship. In other words, because I personally had a revelation of Jesus, I became one of the many living stones in the House of God. "You also, like living stones, are being built into a spiritual house to be a holy priesthood, offering spiritual sacrifices acceptable to God through Jesus Christ" (1 Peter 2:5). The church is not a building. It is a people who have had a revelation that Jesus is the Christ.

As Jacob took his place of *head*ship upon the rock of revelation, God gave him a dream. Let's take another look at the dream.

He saw a *stairway resting on the earth*, with its top reaching to heaven, *and the angels of God were ascending and descending on it*. There *above it stood the LORD*, and he said: 'I am the LORD, the God of your father Abraham and the God of Isaac. I will give you and your descendants the land on which you are lying. Your descendants will be like the dust of the earth, and you will spread out to the west and to the east, to the north and to the south. All peoples on earth will be blessed through you and your offspring. I am with you and will watch over you wherever you go, and I will bring you back to this land. I will not leave you until I have done what I have promised you (Genesis 28:12-15).

Jacob's dream gives us additional insight into various aspects of the church. In the dream he saw a stairway that *rested* on the earth. When you receive a revelation of who Jesus is and what He's done, you can rest in knowing that the rest (peace) of heaven can be yours on earth. God wants His kingdom to come upon the earth just as it is in heaven. Jesus said in Matthew 11:28, "Come to me, all you who are weary and burdened, and I will give you rest."

Before we discuss the angels ascending and descending, I want to look to the top of the ladder. The top reached heaven and above it stood the Lord. Let me say it with a New Covenant perspective. The revelation of Jesus being the Christ will take you to heaven. This revelation grants access to God. It allows you access to God and God access to you. But remember, this dream is taking place *in*side of Jacob. Likewise, for you and I, the dream of having a relationship with the God of creation is only realized *in* Christ Jesus.

Thousands of years later in His dialogue with Nathaniel, Jesus said, "You believe because I told you I saw you under the fig tree. You shall see greater things than that." He then added, "I tell you the truth, you shall see heaven open, and the angels of God ascending and descending on the Son of Man" (John 1:50-51).

Angel literally means, "messenger," and messengers carry messages. These messengers carrying messages may represent literal angelic beings (Daniel 9:21-22, Mark 1:13, Luke 22:43). They may also represent men like you and I who are called to be ambassadors for Christ (2 Corinthians 5:18-20) ascending and descending through the new and living way provided us through Christ (Hebrews 10:19-20). Or, these messengers may simply represent open communication and miracles being transferred between heaven and earth. I believe the latter view is the more appropriate and includes the previous two.

I also believe these revelations are the means by which the prophetic promise to Abraham, Isaac and Jacob will be brought to pass. If you don't have access and specific direction from heaven, then people will not be blessed, spiritual descendants will not be produced, and the promise will not be fulfilled.

It is also important to note, these revelations are made known only in the earth (earthen vessels) in which the Son of Man abides. According to John 1:51, "the angels ascend and descend on the Son of Man," so, if the Son of Man is not in your earth, your earth will not receive revelations from heaven. Jesus, who constantly received specific instruction, only spoke what He heard the Father speak (from heaven) and did only what He saw the Father do (in heaven). We too can receive specific revelation, but it must be based on the rock of revelation that Jesus is the Christ. If you receive a revelation that rests on something other than the lordship of Jesus, then you're climbing up the wrong ladder.

Speaking of a ladder, a ladder has steps. Steps indicate growth and growth is the process of our walk with the Lord, level-to-level and glory-to-glory. In order to grow you have to know how to enter into the presence of the Father. You have to go beyond the veil of things that would distract and cause you to lose focus. You have to enter into the Holy of holies. Messages are best conveyed in person.

Unfortunately, for some of His messengers, they're so far down the stairway it's hard to hear what God is saying. Instead of hearing God's still small voice, God has to yell down the stairway to get their attention. In the troubled times we live, we need messengers who will ascend to the throne of God and come down with a fresh word from heaven. We need men and women who pray and seek God; who receive divinely inspired messages from the Spirit. The world doesn't need another fleshly opinion. We need people who will fall on the rock of revelation of Jesus Christ and then stand up full of the Holy Ghost, having a divine directive for the building of His church.

After Jacob awoke, he realized God had been there and he declared that place to be the house of God, but he also called it something else that gives us another clue that this entire event represents the church. He also called it the gate of heaven. Oh, how little did Jacob know that he was symbolically representing the "gate" into heaven. He was representing Jesus! Jesus said in John 10:9, "I am the gate; whoever enters through me will be saved. He will come in and go out, and find pasture."

Then in response to the revelation Genesis 28:18-19 tells us, "Early the next morning Jacob took the stone he had placed under his head and *set it up as a pillar and poured oil on top of it.* He called that place Bethel, though the city used to be called Luz."

What did Jacob do to the rock? He set it up as a pillar. Here I want you to see this whole thing is a "set up." God has "set you up" to be a pillar in His house. Yes, God has seated you (set you up) in heavenly places (Ephesians 2:6), and 1 Timothy 3:15-16 speaks of "God's household, which is the church of the living God, [as] the *pillar* and foundation of the truth."

The rock is set up and becomes a covenant symbol between him and God. He then pours oil on it. Throughout Scripture oil is a type of the Holy Spirit. What did Jesus pour out upon His church after He ascended to the Father? That's right, the Holy Spirit! This entire picture of Christ's interaction with the church that emerges from the Genesis text revolves around *Jesus/Jacob*. It is all taking place *in, under* and *by Jesus/Jacob*. Again I have to say, "I see Jesus in Jacob!"

Next we go to Genesis 29 where it describes the arrival of Jacob at Paddan Aram where Laban lived. There he came upon some shepherds with their flocks at a well. The well had a large stone over its mouth. It was there that,

> Rachel came with her father's sheep, for she was a shepherdess. When Jacob saw Rachel daughter of Laban, his mother's brother, and Laban's sheep, he (Jacob) went over and *rolled the stone away from the mouth of the well and watered his uncle's sheep.* Then Jacob kissed Rachel and began to weep aloud. He had told Rachel that he was a relative of her father and a son of Rebekah. So she ran and told her father (Genesis 29:9-12).

Thus far we have discussed the "rock of revelation" in reference to the revelation that Jesus is the Christ. Now, we have a picture of another stone and the greatest revelation of Christ's divinity. Jacob rolled away the stone from the mouth of a literal well for Laban's flock to drink. Jesus, on the other hand, had the stone rolled away from the tomb to give living water to the sheep of Israel who had been living under *Laban/Law*.

Mark 16:1-4 says, "Very early on the first day of the week, just after sunrise, they were on their way to the tomb and they asked each other, 'Who will roll the stone away from the entrance of the tomb?' But when they looked up, they saw that *the stone, which was very large, had been rolled away.*"

Then in John 4:13-14 Jesus says, "Everyone who drinks this water will be thirsty again, but *whoever drinks the water I give*

84

him will never thirst. Indeed, the water I give him will become in him a spring of water welling up to eternal life."

The stairway to heaven begins with a rock of revelation and each subsequent revelation takes us from glory to glory. Let's continue on and take the next step in our study because it is about to get exciting. *Jesus/Jacob* is going to get his *Bride/bride*.

ELEVEN

Living Under Laban

"The law was put in charge to lead us to Christ that we might be justified by faith. Now that faith has come, we are no longer under the supervision of the law." - Galatians 3:24-25

The name "Laban" literally means "white." As previously mentioned, *Laban will represent the Law*. When you think about it, it's not too much of a stretch to link a person, (Laban, Moses, or others) with the Law because we know how Jesus is intrinsically linked to the Word. Jesus is the personification of the Word. He is the Word made flesh. He is the fulfillment of all God wanted to say to mankind. Jesus said in Matthew 5:17, "Do not think that I have come to abolish the Law or the Prophets; I have not come to abolish them but to *fulfill* them." In our Genesis text we will continually see how *Jesus/Jacob* fulfills the requirements placed on him by his uncle *Laban/Law*.

Before we get there however, let's examine the bond between these two relatives. Genesis 29:13-14 reads, "As soon as Laban heard *the news* about Jacob, his sister's son, he hurried to meet him. He embraced him and kissed him and brought him to his home, and there Jacob told him all these things. Then Laban said to him, 'You are my own flesh and blood.'"

When Laban heard the *news* that Jacob had come, he hurried to see him. If I were to paraphrase I would say, "When Laban heard the *'good'* news about Jacob." Until Jesus, the Law only brought death. No one could keep it. Finally, there was a man who could keep the commandments, someone who could keep not only the letter, but the spirit of the Law also. Jesus fulfilled it completely, every jot and tittle. Finally, the One who made the Law arrived to live it and show us how to keep it also.

Laban embraced Jacob, kissed him and brought him home. Then it says that Jacob *told him all these things*. This, of course, is referring to Jacob telling Laban about his trip to Paddan Aram, but it reminds me of the many times Jesus said, "You have heard it said, but *I say unto you*." When Jesus came, He came to set the Law straight. Jesus came to explain the true intent of the Law. Jesus came to explain that He had come to fulfill the Law.

Laban/Law makes reference to the bond between he and *Jesus/Jacob* when he says, "You are my own flesh and blood." Actually, when you think about it, Jesus and the Law are one. Jesus is the Word and if part of the Word is the Law, then Jesus is the Law.

Genesis 29:14-15 tells us that, "After Jacob had stayed with him for *a whole month*, Laban said to him, 'Just because you are a relative of mine, should you work for me for nothing? Tell me what your *wages* should be.'"

Typologically the Law is basically saying, "Just because we're related doesn't mean you should work for nothing. You need to get something out of working for (fulfilling) me. What do you want to get out of this?" The wages of breaking the Law (sin) is death, but what are the wages for keeping the Law? The next verse tells us.

"Now Laban had two daughters; the name of the older was Leah, and the name of the younger was Rachel. Leah had weak eyes, but Rachel was lovely in form, and beautiful. Jacob was in

88

love with Rachel and said, 'I'll work for you seven years in return for your younger daughter Rachel'" (Genesis 29:16-18).

Notice that Jacob, not Laban, ultimately determined the duration of his work to be seven years. He would fulfill seven years of labor in return for Laban's daughter Rachel. Jacob loved Rachel. Also notice, Jacob didn't start working for Rachel until he had already stayed with Laban for a whole month. A month is about *thirty* days. And of course, Jesus didn't begin His ministry to the lost sheep of Israel until He was *thirty* years old.

"So Jacob served seven years to get Rachel, but they seemed like only a *few* days to him because of his love for her" (Genesis 29:20).

Jacob served seven years. Seven is the number of completion. Typologically, Jacob *"completed"* his service to get Rachel in what seemed like only a *few* days. It was because of his love for her that he endured his time of service. In the New Testament, it was the joy of getting the Bride (from His own family) that Jesus endured His service (the cross). Then on the *third day (few days) Jesus/Jacob* got Himself a Bride!

Then Jacob said to Laban, "Give me my wife. My time is completed, and I want to lie with her" (Genesis 29:21).

Jacob said, "My time is completed." Jesus said, "It is finished." *Jesus/Jacob* bought his bride with His own sweat and blood. Now He wants to be intimate with her. Now He wants to be fruitful and multiply with her. Now He wants to create a *family/nation* with her.

Jacob loved Rachel just as God loves Israel. 1 Kings 10:9 records the Queen of Sheba speaking to King Solomon of the Lord's love for Israel. "Praise be to the LORD your God, who has delighted in you and placed you on the throne of Israel. Because of *the LORD's eternal love for Israel*, he has made you king, to maintain justice and righteousness." Rachel then, is a type of Israel. Jacob wanted and worked for Rachel just as Jesus wanted and worked for Israel. Israel is the apple of God's eye and God wanted to produce a kingdom through her.

"But when evening came, he [Laban] took his daughter Leah and gave her to Jacob, and Jacob lay with her. And Laban gave his servant girl Zilpah to his daughter as her maidservant. *When morning came, there was Leah*" (Genesis 29:23-25)!

Can someone say, "surprise!" If Rachel is a type of Israel, then whom is Leah a picture of? Weak-eyed Leah has to be a type of the gentiles. The gentiles had been blind to the things of God. The gentiles, like Leah, were alienated and "not loved." So what we see happening is, instead of being intimate with *Rachel/Israel*, it is *Leah/gentiles* who come to *Jesus/Jacob* and begin to produce offspring first. It would be Leah who would cause Rachel to envy. "When Rachel saw that she was not bearing Jacob any children, she became *jealous* of her sister" (Genesis 30:1). The New Testament says, "Through their fall salvation is come unto the Gentiles, for *to provoke them to jealousy*" (Romans 11:11 KJV).

Laban replied to Jacob's complaint by saying, "It is not our custom here to give the younger daughter in marriage before the older one. Finish this daughter's bridal week; then we will give you the younger one also, in return for another seven years of work" (Genesis 29:26-27).

The custom of the land was to give the older daughter in marriage before any of the younger daughters could marry. The gentile unbelievers were in the world before Israel was formed. A covenant creating God's nation of people wasn't made until

Abraham had faith in God's promise. Typologically the gentiles are the older daughter Leah. Israel is the younger daughter Rachel.

Laban then agreed to give Rachel to Jacob once he finished Leah's bridal week. The church period we're currently in is "Leah's bridal week." Jacob will also get *Rachel/Israel*, but he will only get her just before he works for another seven years. Daniel 9:27 tells us that there is one "seven" that remains. It is during this "seven years" that *Rachel/Israel* will be in the spotlight. All eyes will be on Israel again. It is during this seven-year period that Israel will produce for the Kingdom. Completion of the first work for *Laban/Law* brought grace and a gentile church nation. The last "seven years" of work that *Jesus/Jacob* performs will be troublesome, but God will save His people out of it (Jeremiah 30:7). Out of *Jacob's* trouble, He will get both Rachel and Leah.

Romans 11:25-26 says, "Israel has experienced a hardening in part until the full number of the Gentiles has come in. And so all Israel will be saved."

TWELVE

Face the Nation

"I will make you into a great nation and I will bless you; I will make your name great, and you will be a blessing. I will bless those who bless you, and whoever curses you I will curse; and all peoples on earth will be blessed through you." - Genesis 12:2-3

Our text in Genesis 28:31-32 then tells us, "When the LORD saw that *Leah was not loved, he opened her womb,* but *Rachel was barren.* Leah became pregnant and gave birth to a son."

Jacob's nation begins to be formed through Leah. Rachel remained barren. Leah had six sons. Leah's maidservant Zilpah had two sons and Rachel's maidservant Bilah had two sons before Rachel ever conceived. Then Rachel ultimately has two sons rounding out the twelve tribes of Israel.

Genesis 28:32 through 30:24 is the account of the birth of these sons to Jacob. The first thing I want you to consider in this section is that Leah and Rachel's maidservants were given to Jacob to have children with also. Note in particular that the sons birthed through them were just as much a part of the promise as their brothers birthed through Leah and Rachel. Why? This question is especially relevant when in retrospection we remember that Sarah gave Abraham her maidservant Hagar who gave birth to Ishmael, but the promise was not allowed to advance through him. The promise would only be fulfilled through Isaac. Why couldn't the promise have been fulfilled through both Isaac and the handmaiden's child, Ishmael? What's the difference?

Here's a thought to consider. If Abraham is a type of the Father of faith and the only "one" way to see the promises of God manifest in someone's life is by faith, then it would seem appropriate that there be only "one" through whom the promise could come. One child came by the one element necessary to see the promise manifest—faith. The other was a work of the flesh. "For by grace are ye saved *through faith*; and that *not of yourselves*: it is the gift of God: Not of works, lest any man should boast" (Ephesians 2:8-9).

Remember, the arm of the flesh is not an option. You must come to the promise by faith. You can't get to God any other way. "Without faith it is impossible to please God" (Hebrews 11:6). But, *all* who come to *Jesus/Jacob* through that "one" same faith shall be saved.

What's different about Jacob? Jacob is a type of Jesus. *All* who come by faith to Jesus are received. Everyone who unites with Jesus will produce for the Kingdom! John 15:5 says, "If a man remains in me and I in him, he *will* bear much fruit; apart from me you can do nothing."

Romans 10:13, "*Everyone* who calls on the name of the Lord will be saved." You can only come to Jesus by faith, but *all* who do, will receive the promise.

Israel is an Old Covenant type of the New Covenant church. Actually, true Israel is the Church and the true Church is Israel. Neither being born into the natural bloodline nor circumcision of the flesh makes you a true child of Abraham. You must be circumcised of heart. John the Baptist said, "Out of these stones God can raise up children for Abraham" (Matthew 3:9).

The apostle Paul said, "For not all who are descended from Israel are Israel. Nor because they are his descendants are they all Abraham's children" (Romans 9:6-7).

Physically, you have to be born of the bloodline of Jacob to be natural Israel. *Spiritually*, you have to be born by faith into the bloodline of Jesus to be spiritual Israel. I choose the Spirit! If you've been *born again* by the Spirit, you and I are sons and daughters of the promise.

So, if Israel is a type of the church and you and I are the church then typologically that which comprises the foundation of Israel should be evident and foundational in the life of each believer. You are His holy nation! "You are a chosen people, a royal priesthood, a holy nation, a people belonging to God" (1 Peter 2:9).

The twelve sons of Jacob initially made up the nation of Israel. Each one was an element of the whole. What each son represents should also be an essential part of an individual Christian's life as well as our corporate church experience today.

The first son was indeed, "a son." You have to realize that when you become a Christian, you're born into the family of God. You have become the Father's son. When you are born of *Jesus/Jacob*, all of heaven rejoices and says, "*Reuben*." In the original Hebrew language *Reuben means, "Behold a son."* Behold, you have become a *son*.

Galatians 4:4-7 says,

But when the time had fully come, God sent his Son, born of a woman, born under law, to redeem

95

those under law, that we might receive the *full rights* of *sons*. Because *you are sons*, God sent the Spirit of his Son into our hearts, the Spirit who calls out, "Abba, Father." So you are no longer a slave, but a son; and since you are a son, God has made you also an heir.

So again, the first thing that happens to us through *Jesus/Jacob* is that God brings us into His family and makes us a *Reuben/son*. As a Christian you need to have a "Reuben realization" in your life. The knowledge that you are a son will dramatically revolutionize your relationship with God. Before you can see Simeon, Levi or Judah manifest in your life, you must first know Rueben.

Once, however, you know you are a son then you have to come to the understanding of *Simeon*. *Simeon means, "God hears."*

If God loves you enough to make you a son, then He loves you enough to listen to you. The second son Simeon is foundational in Israel, in the church generally, and in you specifically. The fact that God hears us gives us reason to approach Him and speak to Him.

1 John 5:14-15 says, "This is the confidence we have in approaching God: that if we ask anything according to his will, *he hears us.* And *if we know that he hears us* - whatever we ask - we know that we have what we asked of him."

The third son *Levi means, "Joined or Attached."* For you and me to be the family, nation and church God wants us to be, we have to have "Levi" in our lives. We first have to remain *attached* to Jesus. Remember, "apart from me (Jesus) you can do nothing" (John 15:5). We need to stay yoked to Him. Matthew 11:29-30 says, "Take my yoke upon you and learn from me, for I am gentle and humble in heart, and you will find rest for your souls. For my yoke is easy and my burden is light."

Not only do we need to stay attached to Him, but as the *body of Christ*, we also need to stay attached to one another. The Lord's intent is that we who are many members become one. Ephesians 2:21-22 tells us, "In him the whole building is *joined together* and rises to become a holy temple in the Lord. And in him *you too are being built together* to become a dwelling in which God lives by his Spirit."

When you were born into the family, Levi is your brother whether you like it or not. You are joined to brothers and sisters in the Lord. What you do affects others. Being Levi (attached) is part of the Christian experience!

Another important aspect of Levi is how he was attached to both God and his brothers. The Levites became the one tribe among the twelve that served in the house of the Lord. They were the servants and priests in the temple. Today, we have been made a royal priesthood. We are servants of the Most High. To be the greatest in the kingdom of heaven, we must become the servants of all. If you want to stay connected to God and to the Body, it can best be accomplished by *serving*. And again, you must first have these Levi connections before you can legitimately and appropriately have the next son in your life. You must first be joined with God and connected with the Body, and then and only then will you be able to praise the way you are suppose to praise. Look at the importance Jesus places on being properly attached to your brothers before you can properly praise.

"Therefore, if you are offering your gift at the altar and there remember that your brother has something against you, leave your gift there in front of the altar. First go and be reconciled to your brother; then come and offer your gift" (Matthew 5:23-24).

The fourth son of Jacob by his wife Leah was *Judah*. *Judah means, "Praise."* As sons with an attentive Father who has made us *joint*-heirs of His glory, we should and need to praise Him. Appropriate praise comes out of relationship. The praise in turn keeps us attached to the Father, because He inhabits the praises of His people. Judah is a crucial part of the believer's life. It is through Judah the Messiah comes. Jesus is the Lion of Judah.

Do you want Jesus to show up in your situation? Praise! Do you want Him to come forth as a Lion on your behalf? Praise! Do you need a touch from On High? Make Judah a part of your life!

Dan is Jacob's fifth son. *Dan means, "Judge."* As children of God, we are *not* to judge things or people according to the flesh. Matthew 7:1-2 says, "Do not judge, or you too will be judged. For in the same way you judge others, you will be judged, and with the measure you use, it will be measured to you." We are not to judge hypocritically as the context suggests, but we are called upon to make judgments every day. This verse has been taken out of context and used by the devil for too long. Unlike the hypocrites Jesus was talking about, our judgments must be wrapped in love and based in the Word of God.

Dan is a requirement for the believer. We daily have to make judgments. Is something good or bad? Should I do this or that? Will this be beneficial or not? We are even told to determine the true intent and substance of a person by judging the fruit they bear. "Likewise every good tree bears good fruit, but a bad tree bears bad fruit... Thus, by their fruit you will recognize them" (Matthew 7:17-20). In fact, 1 Corinthians 6:2-3 states, "Do you not know that the saints will judge the world? And if you are to judge the world, are you not competent to judge trivial cases? Do you not know that we will judge angels? How much more the things of this life!"

However, before we judge the angels, the world, or the things of this life we must first judge ourselves. "For if we would judge ourselves, we would not be judged" (1 Corinthians 11:31).

As sons we need to be able to judge and discern (Dan) correctly so we can accurately represent the Father's will. Dan, along with all the brothers, is a foundational element of the Christian life.

The next of Jacob's sons is *Naphtali*. *Naphtali means, "My wrestling or My struggle."* Naphtali is the sixth son. Six is the number of man. Six is also the center point on the count to twelve sons. Becoming a Christian does not eliminate struggles. It is actually upon becoming born again that a struggle ensues. Before someone becomes a Christian, the flesh dominates and spiritual concerns are not even dealt with. Whether we like it or not, Naphtali is at the center of every Christian's experience. Although a Christian is born again spiritually, he is still a man. As long as we are living in this flesh, we will always have struggles.

One of the primary struggles a Christian faces is laid out in Romans chapter 7. Romans 7:18-19 says, "For what I do is not the good I want to do; no, the evil I do not want to do-this I keep on doing." So, how do we gain success in this struggle? Paul comes to the conclusion in the same chapter of Romans. Romans 7:24-25 says, "What a wretched man I am! Who will rescue me from this body of death? Thanks be to God -- through Jesus Christ our Lord!" How are we rescued and how do we overcome in this struggle? It is only through Jesus Christ our Lord! Jesus leads us in triumphal procession and causes us to overcome our struggles, but it is in our struggles that we learn to trust in and rely on Jesus. Because of this, we can then have the next son, Gad.

Gad means, "Good fortune." Psalms 23:4-6 says, "Your rod and Your staff, they comfort me. You prepare a table before me in the presence of my enemies; You anoint my head with oil; My cup runs over. Surely *goodness* and mercy shall follow me all the days of my life; And I will dwell in the house of the LORD Forever."

James 1:17 tells us, "Every *good* and perfect gift is from above, coming down from the Father of the heavenly lights."

Truly, every good thing we have is from God. *Good*ness and mercy are to follow the Christian. Wherever you go and whatever you do, you can expect good results. "And we know that in all things God works for the good of those who love him, who have been called according to his purpose" (Romans 8:28).

So, when a Christian begins to walk in his good fortune (Gad), the next son is revealed and he is very, very...

Asher. Asher means, "Happy." Good fortune is an outward influence upon a person, where as happiness is a state of *be*ing. Psalm 68:3 says, "May the righteous be glad and rejoice before God; may they be *happy* and joyful." We have been made the righteousness of Christ, and therefore we have reason to *be* happy. At the same time though, have you ever noticed that everything seems to go well for a happy person? Favor produces happiness, but in turn, happiness produces more favor.

On his deathbed Jacob blessed his eighth son *Asher* by saying, "Bread from Asher shall be rich, and he shall yield royal dainties" (Genesis 49:20). In other words, Asher "happiness" will

100

produce rich bread and royal dainties. Rich and royal are good things so don't worry be happy!

Another point I want to make concerning Asher is that whenever you see the word "blessed" in the Bible it literally means, "happy." So, when you read in Matthew chapter 5, blessed is the poor in spirit, and blessed is the peacemaker, and blessed is the pure in heart, and so on; each of these instances is actually saying, "happy" is the man. When you're blessed, you're happy and when you're happy you're blessed. Asher needs to be a facet of your life.

Noted author and theologian, John Piper has said, "God is most glorified in us when we are most satisfied in Him."[1] In respects to Asher, I would paraphrase by saying, "God is most glorified in us when we are most happy in Him."

So, when you're happy with God and God is happy with you, God will gladly "*Issachar*" you. *Issachar means, "Reward."* Hebrews 11:6 says, "Without faith it is impossible to please God, because anyone who comes to him must believe that he exists and that he *rewards* those who earnestly seek him."

Salvation is by grace alone. You can do nothing to earn it lest any man should boast. But, ultimate rewards are based on what you do. Revelation 22:12 tells us, "Behold, I am coming soon! My *reward* is with me, and *I will give to everyone according to what he has done.*"

Part of the Issachar reward will be the very presence of God as He comes to *dwell* with you and grant you great *honor* in His Kingdom.

Zebulun is the tenth of Jacob's sons and the last son of Leah. *Zebulun means, "Dwelling or Honor."* Again I'll quote from the 23rd Psalm. "Surely goodness and mercy shall follow me all the days of my life; and I will *dwell* in the house of the LORD forever." The father in the story of the prodigal son said to the older brother who stayed home, "My son you are always with me, and everything I have is yours" (Luke 15:31).

When you dwell with the Lord, not only does the Father give you good fortune, make you happy, and give you great rewards, but He also gives you complete access to all that is His on an ongoing basis, simply on the grounds that you *dwell* together with Him. You can go to the refrigerator when you want. You can go to the closet or the medicine cabinet, as you need. You can play in the yard, or kick your feet up on the coffee table and rest in the Comforter. No good thing will He withhold from you.

Then, when you think you have everything you need and there couldn't be anymore to be gained or attained, there's *Joseph*. Joseph is the first son of Rachael, who we've been using as a type of Israel. *Joseph means, "God adds or increases."* Psalm 23 says, "My cup runneth over." When you can't hold anymore, God's not finished yet. He just keeps on pouring.

One of my favorite verses tells us, "He will be called Wonderful Counselor, Mighty God, Everlasting Father, Prince of Peace. Of the *increase* of his government and peace *there will be no end"* (Isaiah 9:6-7).

This verse tells us His Kingdom of peace will always and forever be increasing and advancing. I cannot even begin to imagine how this will happen, but it seems to indicate that God will include us in the advancement of His government to a limitless extent. He wants to advance His Kingdom throughout eternity, but He also wants to increase His territory and His sphere of influence in you and through you now! Don't let the pressures of this world put a squeeze on the Kingdom in you. Jabez prayed it: "Oh, that you would bless me and enlarge my territory" (1 Chronicles 4:10)! Joseph (God increases) is an element you can expect in your Christian experience. There is more.

Finally, we have the birth of Jacob's youngest son *Benjamin* recorded in Genesis 35:18-24. During the birth process Rachel died. As she lay dying she named the child *Ben-Oni, which means "Son of my pain,"* but *Jacob renamed him Benjamin, which means "Son of my right hand."*

Although we've caused God much grief and hurt, and although the only solution to our sin problem was for God to sacrifice His Son, and although Jesus had to suffer great physical and emotional *pain* in going to the cross, it was for the joy of seeing many sons made strong in Him that He endured it all. Suffering, pain, and death are finished in Him. It is finished and we are made strong in the power of His might!

He no longer calls you Ben-Oni "son of my pain," but instead *He calls you "Son of my strength."* The right hand is a symbol of strength. *When we are weak, He is shown strong.* God will take every pain you've gone through, turn it around, rename it and cause it to make you stronger. The pain and difficulties you are facing are not designed to destroy you, but rather to define and strengthen you. You will be an overcomer. Ultimately, you and I will sit at His right hand as the *body of Christ.* In fact, positionally we are already there. We are seated with Christ in the heavenly places. "God raised us up with Christ and seated us with him in the heavenly realms in Christ Jesus" (Ephesians 2:6).

Both Joseph and Benjamin were children born of Rachel (our type of Israel) and although they were the last to be born, they each held a special place in *Jesus/Jacob's* heart. Joseph was given a special coat and was the possessor of a dream that would be key to the whole family's deliverance from *seven* years of a severe and troubling famine. And, before the entire nation could be saved by a great deliverance, Benjamin, the youngest, had to be sent by *Jesus/Jacob* into Egypt. Then the whole family was able to enjoy the fat of the land (Genesis 45:7, 18-19). I believe our ability as a church to rule and reign in this world (Egypt) hinges upon Leah's children (gentile believers) and Rachael's children (Jewish believers) embracing and accepting one another, so we may all eat of the good of the land.

The twelve attributes represented by each of the twelve sons of Jacob need to be realized on an ever-increasing basis personally in an individual's life as well as corporately in the body of Christ as a whole. They will only fully manifest, however, when we get to Revelation 21:9-13.

> "'Come, I will show you the bride, the wife of the Lamb.' And he carried me away in the Spirit to a mountain great and high, and showed me the Holy City, Jerusalem, coming down out of heaven from God. It shone with the glory of God, and its brilliance was like that of a very precious jewel, like a jasper, clear as crystal. It had a great, high wall with twelve gates, and with twelve angels at the gates. *On the gates were written the names of the twelve tribes of Israel.*"

In Revelation 21, we see how the twelve elements of the Christian experience become *gates* for us to go in and out from the presence of God. One day, we may literally go into the presence of God through *Rueben/Behold a son,* and be sent out through *Asher/Happy.*

MEANING of NAMES
and
ELEMENTS of the CHRISTIAN LIFE

Rueben - "Behold a son"   **Simeon** - "God hears"
Levi - "Joined/Attached"   **Judah** - "Praise"
Dan - "Judge"   **Naphtali** - "My struggle"
Gad - "Good fortune"   **Asher** - "Happy"
Issachar - "Reward"   **Zebulun** - "Dwelling/Honor"
Joseph - "God increases"   **Benjamin** - "Son of my
                                              right hand"

[1] Dr. John Piper, *Desiring God: Meditations of a Christian Hedonist* (Portland: Multnomah Press, 1986), p. 50.

THIRTEEN

Flock to Jacob

"Rejoice with me; I have found my lost sheep." - Luke 15:6

The twelve sons were the initial founders of the nation that God is building. Through the years they would truly multiply and grow to become a nation of people. We have just finished looking at each of Jacob's sons, but now beginning in verse 25 of chapter 30, we will see how Jacob, at God's command, begins to lead his wives and children out from a life of living under *Laban/Law*. Jacob is going to bring those who are his, to his father. He wants to take his bride and his children home.

Laban resists Jacob's request and basically says that he can name his wages if he stays. Laban realizes that it is because of Jacob that the Lord has blessed him. Jacob also recognizes that Laban is being blessed because of him and responds to Laban by saying, "The little you had before I came has increased greatly, and the LORD has blessed you wherever I have been" (Genesis 30:30).

This is true for you and me also. The only reason we are blessed is a result of Jesus. The only way the Law can bless someone is because Jesus has fulfilled it. You can't work for *Laban/Law* hard enough or long enough to be blessed. It's in and through *Jesus/Jacob* that blessing and increase come, not by keeping the Law. Do you want to be blessed in life? Stop trying to keep the Law, and instead, get close to Jesus—that's where the blessings are, and He is how you keep the Law.

Knowing where the blessing has been coming from, Laban continues to insist, "What shall I give you?"

"Don't give me anything," Jacob replied. "But if you will do this one thing for me, I will go on tending your flocks and watching over them: Let me go through all your flocks today and remove from them every speckled or spotted sheep, every dark colored lamb and every spotted or speckled goat. *They will be my wages*" (Genesis 30:31-32).

Praise God! *Jacob took every spotted and speckled sheep.* Again the type is beautiful. Jacob went through and made every dark colored and spotted sheep his own. This is exactly what Jesus did! I am one of the speckled sheep. Although I am tainted with sin and spotted with the filth of this world, Jesus came and found me, called me by name, and chose me to be in His flock. I have become a sheep of His pasture.

Jesus said it this way, "It is not the healthy who need a doctor, but the sick. I have not come to call the righteous, but sinners" (Mark 2:17). Hallelujah! The spotted sheep were the wages of his labor. He worked that we might have rest and lay down in green pastures.

Laban agreed to Jacob's proposal. Next, I want you to see the separation that occurs and what Jacob does. Look at Genesis 30:36-43:

> Then he put a *three-day* journey between himself and Jacob, while Jacob continued to tend the rest of Laban's flocks. Jacob, however, took fresh-cut *branch*es from poplar, almond and plane trees and made *white stripes* on them by peeling the bark and *exposing the white* inner wood of the branches. Then he placed the peeled branches in all the

watering troughs, so that they would be directly in front of the flocks when they *came to drink*. When the flocks were in heat and came to drink, they mated in front of the branches. And they bore young that were streaked or speckled or spotted. Jacob set apart the young of the flock by themselves, but made the rest face the streaked and dark-colored animals that belonged to Laban. Thus he made separate flocks for himself and did not put them with Laban's animals. Whenever the stronger females were in heat, Jacob would place the branches in the troughs in front of the animals so they would mate near the branches, but if the animals were weak, he would not place them there. So *the weak animals went to Laban and the strong ones to Jacob*. In this way *the man grew exceedingly prosperous and came to own large flocks*, and maidservants and menservants, and camels and donkeys.

The separation between *Laban/Law* and *Jesus/Jacob* was a *three-day journey*. This too is what brought us from having to live under the Law to the place of living under grace. Within a *three-day* span of time all mankind went from being hopeless captives to the Law to having the hope of being raised with Christ. We now have hope in the One who redeemed us from the curse of the Law (Galatians 3:13). He purchased us that we might belong to Him. He laid down His life so we could live!

Jacob made stripes on branches to expose the white wood within. He placed these at the watering troughs. When the sheep came to drink they would mate in front of the branches and they would bear young that were speckled and spotted, and they would belong to Jacob.

109

Let's look at some Scripture. "A shoot will come up from the stump of Jesse; from his roots a *Branch* will bear fruit. The Spirit of the LORD will rest on him" (Isaiah 11:1-2).

"The days are coming," declares the LORD, "when I will raise up to David a righteous *Branch*, a King who will reign wisely and do what is just and right in the land. In his days Judah will be saved and Israel will live in safety. This is the name by which he will be called: The LORD Our Righteousness" (Jeremiah 23:5-6).

"I am going to bring my servant, the *Branch*... and I will remove the sin of this land in a single day" (Zechariah 3:8-9).

Each of these texts refers to a Branch who is none other than Jesus. The branches here in our Genesis study can be viewed as another picture of the Messiah. This story is just brimming with Jesus. Jesus was the Branch who bore stripes upon His back for our sins, our spots (1 Peter 2:24). He had no sin of His own. He was "white" within. He was the pure and spotless "white within" sacrifice. Keep in mind, Laban's name means, "white." *Jacob/Jesus/Word* fulfilled *Laban/Law/Word*.

So, when the sheep were thirsty they came and stood before the exposed Branch. Jesus said in John 7:37, "If anyone is thirsty, let him come to me and drink."

If you want to be filled, then you need to come to Jesus. If you want to produce offspring and make disciples for the Kingdom, you need to come to Jesus. If you want to be strong in the things of God, then you need to come to the Branch!

Remember, our text says the weak animals went to Laban and the strong to Jacob. Saints of God, be strong in the Lord and in the power of His might! Don't rely on the weak arm of the flesh to attempt keeping laws, rituals and customs according to your own strength. *Let the weak say, I am strong!*

Beginning in chapter 31 of Genesis we read that *Laban's sons* began saying something very interesting. Laban's sons realized, "Jacob has taken everything our father owned and has gained all this wealth from what belonged to our father." This is amazing! *All the Law was fulfilled and now all its promises fully belong to Christ.* All the Law intended to do, but couldn't, was done by Jesus. All the benefits and promises attached to keeping the Law now belong to Jesus. Everything the Law had to offer is now found in Him!

Next, in Genesis 31:3-13, we are given some insight as to who was behind Jacob's great increase and blessing.

> Then the *LORD said* to Jacob, "*Go back to the land of your fathers* and to your relatives, and *I will be with you.*" So Jacob sent word to Rachel and Leah to come out to the fields where his flocks were. He said to them, "I see that your father's attitude toward me is not what it was before, but *the God of my father has been with me.* You know that *I've worked for your father with all my strength*, yet your father has cheated me by changing my wages *ten times. However, God has not allowed him to harm me.* If he said, 'The *speckled ones* will be your wages,' *then all the flocks gave birth to speckled young*; and *if he said*, 'The *streaked ones* will be your wages,' then all the flocks bore *streaked young. So God has taken away your father's livestock and has given them to me.* "In breeding season I once had *a dream* in which I looked up and saw that the male goats mating with the flock were streaked, speckled or spotted. 11 *The*

111

*angel of God said to me in the dream, 'Jacob.' I
answered, 'Here I am.' 12 And he said, 'Look up
and see that all the male goats mating with the flock
are streaked, speckled or spotted, for I have seen all
that Laban has been doing to you.* 13 I am the God
of Bethel, where you anointed a pillar and where
you made a vow to me. *Now leave this land at once
and go back to your native land.'"*

It had been God leading Jacob the whole time. This was
not some elaborate scheme that Jacob had come up with on his
own to swindle the flock from Laban. No, this was God's hand of
blessing upon him. This was God giving Jacob insight on how to
prosper. This was God giving us a picture of the Good Shepherd
taking stripes upon His back in order to gain a flock. Also notice
that it was Laban who changed the requirements that needed to be
met in order for Jacob to earn his wages. He did this *ten times.*
This reminds me of the Ten Commandments. It is a picture that
shows us no matter what demands the Law tries to impose Jesus
has it covered. Jesus will take those who have served other gods,
disobeyed their parents, or murdered. If you come to the Branch
and His watering trough, He will make you His.

Then Rachel and Leah replied to Jacob, "Do we still have
any share in the inheritance of our father's estate? Does he not
regard us as foreigners? Not only has he sold us, but he has used
up what was paid for us. Surely *all the wealth that God took away
from our father belongs to us and our children.* So do whatever
God has told you" (Genesis 31:14-16).

This verse shows us that when you are in relationship with
Jesus/Jacob, and if you are born of Him, what belongs to Him
becomes yours also. All the Law had to offer now belongs to
Jesus, and if you are in relationship with Him, it also belongs to

you too by virtue of your position in Him! In this light, I think it is appropriate to read Deuteronomy 28:1-14.

> If you *fully obey* the LORD your God and carefully follow *all his commands* I give you today, *the LORD your God will* set you high above all the nations on earth. *All these blessings will come upon you and accompany you* if you obey the LORD your God: You will be blessed in the city and blessed in the country. The fruit of your womb will be blessed, and the crops of your land and the young of your livestock — the calves of your herds and the lambs of your flocks. Your basket and your kneading trough will be blessed. You will be blessed when you come in and blessed when you go out. The LORD will grant that the enemies who rise up against you will be defeated before you. They will come at you from one direction but flee from you in seven. The LORD will send a blessing on your barns and on everything you put your hand to. The LORD your God will bless you in the land he is giving you. The LORD will establish you as his holy people, as he promised you on oath, if you keep the commands of the LORD your God and walk in his ways. Then all the peoples on earth will see that you are called by the name of the LORD, and they will fear you. The LORD will grant you abundant prosperity — in the fruit of your womb, the young of your livestock and the crops of your ground — in the land he swore to your forefathers to give you. The LORD will open the heavens, the storehouse of his bounty, to send rain on your land in season and to bless all the work of your hands. You will lend to many nations but will borrow from none. The LORD will make you the head, not the

tail. If you pay attention to the commands of the LORD your God that I give you this day and carefully follow them, you will always be at the top, never at the bottom. Do not turn aside from any of the commands I give you today, to the right or to the left, following other gods and serving them.

All of this can be yours, not because you can fully obey the Law, but because Jesus did. It is Jesus alone who has fully obeyed the Law of God. This is why we must stay in relationship with Him!

Once everything belonging to *Laban/Law* became *Jesus/Jacob's*, look again at what the Lord says. "Then the LORD said to Jacob, 'Go back to the land of your fathers and to your relatives, and I will be with you'" (Genesis 31:3). We find in verse 13, this command was to be obeyed "at once."

It's time to get out from under the Law! It is not by works that you are saved, lest any man should boast (Ephesians 2:9). Jacob gathers Rachel and Leah and it says that "Jacob put his children and his wives on camels, and he drove all his livestock ahead of him, along with all the goods he had accumulated in Paddan Aram, to go to his father Isaac in the land of Canaan" (Genesis 31:17-18). Laban cried deception (Genesis 31:26), but Scripture claims it was obedience.

They're headed for the Promised Land, the land flowing with milk and honey. Promised Land living can't be found by living under the Law, but Jesus will take you there!

Everything is going great. Jacob is proceeding according to plan. His family is going along with the arrangement. But then "When Laban had gone to shear his sheep, Rachel stole her father's household gods" (Genesis 31:19).

114

Trouble in paradise! Jesus has saved us and set us free, but what happens when you let sin in the camp? Well, what we see happening next is Laban heading out after Jacob and his family. Laban catches up to those going with Jacob and he asks; "Now you have gone off because you longed to return to your father's house. But why did you steal my gods" (Genesis 31:30)?

First of all, if Laban is a type of the Law, and Laban has these "gods" he shouldn't have, what might they represent? Could we consider these "gods" a type of what we many times add to the Law that shouldn't be there? Could these "gods" possibly represent the "traditions of men?" Believe me, there are certainly some "traditions of men" that are added to the Law that people like Rachel grab hold of and don't want to leave behind.

Laban/Law accuses Jacob of stealing his idols, but it was not Jacob who stole them. It was Rachel. Jacob tells Laban that if he finds anyone among his nation with the idols, that person would be put to death. The wages of sin is still death. All who break the Law of Laban by holding on to idols deserve death. So, what happens to Rachel? Do they take her out and stone her?

Genesis 31:34-35 reads, "Now Rachel had taken the household gods and put them inside her camel's saddle and was sitting on them. Laban searched through everything in the tent but *found nothing*. Rachel said to her father, 'Don't be angry, my lord, that I cannot stand up in your presence; I'm having my period.' So he searched but could not find the household gods."

You and I, and Rachel are law-breakers. We deserve death. It is *Laban/Law* who points this out to us. Just as Rachel could not stand up in the presence of *Laban/Law* neither can you or I, or we would be found guilty. As you know, we fall far too short. We can't stand against the standard. In addition to being law-breakers, we cannot stand up because our blood is unclean. Sin is in our

115

blood. However, because Rachael is in relationship with *Jesus/Jacob* she is no longer under the curse. When you and I belong to Jesus, His (red soup) blood covers our transgressions. It is the untainted blood of Jesus that covers the sins in our saddlebags. Jacob was Rachel's covering and Jesus is ours.

Jacob then asks Laban, "What sin have I committed that you hunt me down? Now that you have searched through all my goods, what have you found that belongs to your household? Put it here in front of your relatives and mine, and let them judge between the two of us" (Genesis 31:36-37).

Rachel was guilty, but Jacob was not. Rachel sinned, but Jacob had committed no sin. This is why Jesus' blood covers! His death met the requirements of God. There was no sin found in Him! He was white within. Therefore, His sacrifice was accepted once and for all. His blood doesn't cover for a year and then another sacrifice has to be made. No! His work is complete. He has taken us out from under the bondage of the Law, and He is now sitting at the right hand of the Father, and as His Body, we're seated with Him.

Jacob goes on to say to Laban, "I did not bring you animals torn by wild beasts; *I bore the loss myself.* And you demanded payment from me for whatever was stolen by day or night" (Genesis 31:39).

The devil and legalistic religion are thieves who come to steal, kill and destroy (John 10:10). If you find yourself torn up over something, or a situation you are going through has *stolen* your joy, don't place yourself deeper in a rut by thinking, "things aren't the same; He'll never use me; I'll never do anything for God; I've fallen and I can't get up." No! The Law can't find your failure because the blood covers it. God doesn't even know a loss has been incurred because *Jesus/Jacob bore the loss Himself.* He

116

made up for it. And now in Christ, you stand justified—just as if you never sinned.

He absorbed the cost. He paid the price for everything that had been stolen and now *everything the devil has stolen can be found in Christ!*

Next, Laban and Jacob make a covenant with each other. Genesis 31:44-52 records Laban as saying,

'Come now, let's make a covenant, you and I, and let it serve as a witness between us.' Laban also said to Jacob, 'Here is this heap, and here is this pillar I have set up between you and me. This heap is a witness, and this pillar is a witness, that I will not go past this heap to your side to harm you and that you will not go past this heap and pillar to my side to harm me.'

Jesus/Jacob came not to abolish *Laban/Law*, but to fulfill it. Jesus has not come to harm the Law, but neither should the Law try to cross over to impede upon or harm grace. Anytime the boundary is breeched it should only be for the purpose of blessing and not harm. For example the Law may pass over into grace to bring about a more dedicated and disciplined lifestyle. You just shouldn't impose or harm others with your personal parameters. On the other hand, grace at times may pass over into the Law in order to love or live. Examples may include: healing on the Sabbath (John 9:14), eating the showbread (1 Samuel 21:6), or eating meat that has been sacrificed to idols (1 Corinthians 10:25, 26). "Be careful, however, that the exercise of your freedom does not become a stumbling block to the weak" (1 Corinthians 8:9). Keep in mind; the weak are those who went to *Laban/Law*.

"So Jacob took an oath in the name of the Fear of his father Isaac. *He offered a sacrifice there in the hill country and invited his relatives to a meal.* After they had eaten, they spent the night there. Early the next morning Laban kissed his grandchildren and his daughters and blessed them. Then he left and returned home" (Genesis 31:53-55).

Here again we see a beautiful picture of Jesus fulfilling the oath between He and His Father by offering Himself as a sacrifice on a *hill* called Calvary. Now *you are invited* to partake of the meal He has provided.

FOURTEEN

God Grasper

"If only there were someone to arbitrate between us, to lay his hand upon us both, someone to remove God's rod from me..."
- Job 9:33-34

At this point I am going to skip ahead a little bit in our story and come back in the next section to discuss the material I'm passing over. I'm doing this so I can complete the picture of the sacrifice *Jesus/Jacob* has made.

We were first introduced to Jacob holding on to the heel of his brother Esau.

This is what Jesus did for us. Man needed to be reached, so Jesus, in His humanity, held on to sinful man. He wouldn't let us go. He wouldn't leave us to ourselves. Jesus associated with us. He felt our pain and our suffering. He even died our death. He received our punishment. He *heeled/healed* us.

So, we've seen Jesus grasping Adam's heel. There remains, however, one crucial element that has to be discussed. The question that has to be asked is—in His association with man did Jesus ever let go of God?

Maybe at His weakest moment, maybe just once, He let go. If this were true, we would all be lost forever, separated by a gulf of sin. But, perhaps once in His frailty He loosened the standard and compromised just a little.

Yes, He felt our emotions. He felt the cold we feel at night and the heat of the noonday sun. He felt thirsty after a full day's work. He did associate with man's weakness, but He never sinned. Although He was tempted in every way common to man, yet He sinned not. *He continued to hold on to God!*

Let me show you:

That night Jacob got up and took his two wives, his two maidservants and his eleven sons and crossed the ford of the Jabbok. After he had sent them across the stream, he sent over all his possessions. So Jacob was left *alone*, and a man wrestled with him till daybreak. When the man saw that he could not overpower him, he touched the socket of Jacob's hip so that his hip was wrenched as he wrestled with the man. Then the man said, 'Let me go, for it is daybreak.' But Jacob replied, 'I will not let you go unless you bless me.' The man asked him, 'What is your name?' 'Jacob,' he answered. Then the man said, 'Your name will no longer be Jacob, but Israel, because *you have struggled with God and with men and have overcome.*'

Here in Genesis 32:22-28 is the account of Jacob wrestling with God, but when did Jesus "wrestle" with God? Well, let's look at the most obvious.

Luke 22:41-44 says,

He withdrew about a stone's throw beyond them, knelt down and prayed, 'Father, if you are willing,

120

take this cup from me; *yet not my will, but yours be done.*' An angel from heaven appeared to him and strengthened him. And *being in anguish*, he prayed more earnestly, and his sweat was like drops of blood falling to the ground.

Here, Jesus and His Father are *alone* talking with one another. The Father's will seems harsh, and Jesus is in great anguish over it. This is the wrestling match that goes on in each one of us. This was the struggle in Rebekah's womb between Jacob and Esau. And yes, because He put on flesh, Jesus had this struggle too.

The "man" in the Genesis text, who is actually God, touches Jacob's hip and wrenches it out of place, but still Jacob holds on. The hip is the center of strength and the area of productivity.

The nation of Israel thought the Messiah would come as a gallant conquering king. Instead, He was born in a manger; He was born in weakness and came meek and mild riding on the foal of a donkey. Jesus didn't save the world when He came out of the wilderness in the power of the Holy Spirit. It wasn't when He was at the apex of His healing ministry; when the blind were receiving their sight, the lame were walking, and even the dead were rising that Jesus saved the world. No—Jesus saved the world when He was at His weakest. He saved the world when He was beaten, scourged, and hung on a tree with nails through hands and feet. He didn't save the world when He fed the 5,000 and had multitudes of followers. He saved the world when He was by Himself—*alone* and naked, bleeding, and hanging between heaven and earth, hanging *between God and man.*

He wrestled with God and He wrestled with man and *He prevailed* (Genesis 32:28)!

Jesus/Jacob's hip had been touched. He took upon Himself the limp of humanity. He felt the utter weakness of man, yet He would not let go of God. He did not let go! He finished the work, and He received His blessing.

Job says in Job 9:33, "If only there were someone to arbitrate between us, to lay his hand upon us both." Well Job, I have good news. Now there is someone! Jesus could touch man because He was man and He could touch God because He was God. He is the God-man, Christ Jesus. He is the one who reached out His arms on an old rugged cross and became the mediator, the arbitrator between the two.

Job needed an arbitrator, but Scripture also records in Ezekiel's day that God, "looked for a man among them who would build up the wall and stand before me in the gap on behalf of the land so I would not have to destroy it, but I found none" (Ezekiel 22:30).

God also needed a mediator to get what He wanted. God didn't want to bring destruction upon the land. He wants to bring life. God is the author of life, not the destroyer of it. Destruction only comes to that which is already dead. Everyone who does not have God does not have life. Oh, the chasm, the gulf, the separation! Who can bridge the gap between God and man? Now there is One! Now, the Way-maker has become the Way.

It is because of the cross we can cross the great divide and reach God. It is because of the cross that God can once again step into our lives and heal our land, our earthen vessels.

Hidden within Jacob's story is the story of the bridging of that great gulf. We have followed *Jesus/Jacob* from the time he held on to *Edom/man* to the point where he holds on to God, and now *Jesus/Jacob* possesses every blessing that can be possessed.

He has prevailed! He has won the victory!

God has placed *everything* under His feet. He has crushed the head of the enemy. *Jesus Christ is Lord!* "Jesus came to them and said, 'All authority in heaven and on earth has been given to me'" (Matthew 28:18). Now, if Jesus has won the victory, then you and I are also victorious in Him!

Next, Jacob gets a name change. God changes his name from "heel grasper" to "Israel." *Israel means, "Prince with God, or Having power with God, or God's fighter."* *Jesus/Jacob* goes from a son of weakness to son of power. The physical body of Jesus; the incarnate Christ who was also the firstborn of many brothers [was] sown [into the earth] as perishable, it [his body] [was] raised imperishable; it [was] sown in dishonor, it [was] raised in glory; it [was] sown in weakness, it [was] raised in power; it [was] sown a natural body, it [was] raised a spiritual body (1 Corinthians 15:42-44, present tense switched to past tense parentheses mine).

Jesus is both our Jacob and our Israel. He is our Savior and our Lord. Jesus is our Heal Grasper and our Prince with God. He became like us and bore the limp of humanity so we could become like Him and bear His image in glory! "By his power God *raised* the Lord from the dead, and *he will raise us also*" (1 Corinthians 6:14).

The perishable putting on the imperishable in 1 Corinthians chapter 15:42-44 paraphrased above actually refers to Jesus returning to receive His own. At that time we will see Him face to face and we will be changed. "We know that when he appears, we shall be like him, for we shall see him as he is" (1 John 3:2). *Jesus/Jacob* is returning. He will meet *Esau/flesh* someday. The question is, "Is your *Esau/flesh* ready to receive Him?"

123

FIFTEEN

Face to Face

"...then we shall see face to face. Now I know in part; then I shall know fully, even as I am fully known." - 1 Corinthians 13:12

Genesis 32:3-4 says "Jacob sent messengers ahead of him to his brother Esau in the land of Seir, the country of Edom. He instructed them: 'This is what you are to say...'"

Jacob sent messengers and gifts ahead of his arrival to the country of *Edom/Adam*, and so has Jesus. Jesus told His messengers, the disciples, to go into all the world (to the Esaus of the world), and to preach the good news. "Whoever believes and is baptized will be saved, but whoever does not believe will be condemned" (Mark 16:15-16).

It goes on further to tell us,

From what he had with him he selected a gift for his brother Esau: two hundred female goats and twenty male goats... *He put them in the care of his servants*, each herd by itself, and said to his servants, "*Go ahead of me*, and keep some space between the herds." He instructed the one in the lead: When my brother Esau meets you and asks, 'To whom do you belong, and where are you going, and who owns all these animals in front of you?' then you are to say, '*They belong to your servant Jacob*. They are a gift

sent to my lord Esau, and *he is coming* behind us'
(Genesis 32:13-18).

Now look at the incredible parallels that can be drawn from these verses in Genesis when compared with Ephesians 4:8-13:

When he ascended on high, he led captives in his train and *gave gifts to men...* It was he who *gave* some to be apostles, some to be prophets, some to be evangelists, and some to be pastors and teachers, *to prepare God's people* for works of service, so that the body of Christ may be built up *until we all* reach unity in the faith and in the knowledge of the Son of God and *become mature*, attaining to the whole measure of the *fullness of Christ*.

Jacob wanted to be sure all those he sent ahead of him were to say, "'your servant Jacob is coming behind us.' For he thought, 'I will pacify him with these gifts I am sending on ahead; later, when I see him, *perhaps he will receive me.*' So Jacob's gifts went on ahead of him...'" (Genesis 32:20-21).

Well, let me go *ahead* and tell you; Jesus has sent me on *ahead* of His imminent arrival. He is right behind me. He is on His way. He's coming soon!

I am just a messenger, crying out in the wilderness, "Prepare ye the way of the Lord!" The Lord is coming back! I belong to the Lord and the fullness of the earth is His. He owns the cattle on a thousand hills, and all that you see belongs to Him. I'm going to those who afar off to preach the news that the Kingdom is near. He has sent me and has provided many good gifts in hopes that you might receive Him.

In Genesis 33:4 it says that Esau ran to meet Jacob and embraced him; he threw his arms around his neck and kissed him. And they wept.

This is such a beautiful picture. Oh, how we need Jesus! Oh, how we need to run to Him and embrace Him. There are many *Esaus* today who need to embrace Him. There may be someone you know who has only known the flesh, but today is his or her day to embrace the divine. Esau, it's time to give up your fleshy ways and it's time to receive *Jesus/Jacob*. All have been born into the flesh, but today is the day to be born again in Christ.

Finally Esau asked,

'What do you mean by all these droves I met?' 'To find favor in your eyes, my lord,' Jacob said. But Esau said, 'I already have plenty, my brother. Keep what you have for yourself.' 'No, please!' said Jacob. 'If I have found favor in your eyes, accept this gift from me. *For to see your face is like seeing the face of God, now that you have received me favorably.* Please accept the present that was brought to you, for God has been gracious to me and I have all I need.' And *because Jacob insisted, Esau accepted it*' (Genesis 33:8-11).

Again, Jesus has given us salvation, He has poured out the Holy Spirit, He has also sent apostles, prophets, evangelists, pastors and teachers, and He has given us everything that pertains to life and godliness so people might look favorably upon Him. "God's kindness leads you toward repentance" (Romans 2:4). Accept His gifts. Accept what He's provided for you. He insists on it. Although you may have plenty on your own, you don't have enough. You need what Jesus has! Others of you may have thought you forfeited the blessing because of the things you've done in your past, but right now Jesus is offering you the very blessing you thought you lost. Even though you have chosen the Esau way all your life, you can accept *Jesus/Jacob's* blessing today.

Jacob then makes this interesting statement; it bears repeating: *to see your face is like seeing the face of God, now that you have received me favorably.* Let me clarify the progression as He speaks to Esau. He said, now that you have received me or since you have received me—I look at you and it's like seeing the face of God. Did you get that?

Trying to trap Jesus, the Pharisees asked Him if it were right to pay taxes to Caesar or not. Jesus' response of course, was perfect. He had them show Him a coin used for paying the tax. Then He asked, "Whose portrait is this? And whose inscription?" "Caesar's," they replied. Then He told them, "Give to Caesar what is Caesar's, and to God what is God's" (Mark 12:17).

In other words, they could give the coin to Caesar, but man who bears the image of God belongs to God. You and I were created in the image and likeness of God. We are His. Unfortunately, due to sin, our image has been marred and disfigured from its original design. The devil lied when he told Adam and Eve they had to eat of the tree of the knowledge of good and evil to become like God (Genesis 3:5). This inferred they were not like Him, but the truth was; they were. That was the lie. They already bore God's image. Adam despised and therefore lost all he had because he thought it was necessary to gain something that already belonged to him. So again, because of their sin, the image became tainted and only a part of what it used to be.

The Genesis account of Jacob shows us there is hope. Once we have been born into Adam and have lived like Esau, our hope; our only hope lies in favorably receiving *Jesus/Jacob*. Once we receive His messengers and thereby favorably receive Him (Matthew 10:40), there will come a day when we will see Him face to face. There is coming a day when our perishable shall put on the imperishable and our dishonor shall be changed to glory. "For those God foreknew he also predestined to be conformed to the likeness of his Son, that he might be the firstborn among many brothers" (Romans 8:29).

We are destined to once again look like Him! One day Jesus will be able to say when He looks at us that it's like looking at Himself. The fraternal shall become identical. And whom does Jesus look like?

Jesus told Philip in John 14.9, "*If you have seen me you have seen the Father.*" When we see Jesus face to face and are changed into His image, we too will look like the Father. As Jacob said, "To see your face is like seeing the face of God." There will be a day when we will look like we should. There will be a day when the image and likeness we were created in will be restored. There will be a day when we will be holy as He is holy. There will be a day when we look like our Father. There will be a day when we grow up and become mature in Christ, and the second-born Adam who became our firstborn brother will step back from our embrace to look at us and say, "It's good to see you my brother; and you look so much like Dad!" Oh, what a day that will be when my Jesus I shall see!

This is such great news because it appeared to be a hopeless situation for Esau. It didn't look like he would ever make a right decision. Finally however, Esau comes to a point where he gets past his jealousy and gets past his flesh, and he receives both the birthright and the blessing he always wanted *by receiving Jacob.* When Esau embraced Jacob, he was embracing the promise. He was uniting himself with the one whom God loved. The blessing Jacob gained while living under Laban was sent on ahead to Esau. Jacob insisted Esau receive it. We too were hopeless, but once we receive Jesus, we receive abundant life, peace beyond understanding, and joy unspeakable and full of glory. We receive love, power, and a sound mind! We receive all the benefits of salvation full and free!

Esau, the secret to receiving *Jesus/Jacob's* blessing is to receive *Jesus/Jacob*. Receive the gift of Jesus today! This is how you become the complete person God intends for you to be. You must embrace the substitutionary and atoning work of Christ in order for you to be justified. You must embrace Jesus' fulfillment of the Law in order for you to get the flesh out, and become a person who is sanctified and set apart for the Lord. And, you must embrace the fact that Jesus has all you need, and is all you need, in order for you to be glorified with Him forever.

The Genesis account of Jacob continues, but the type begins to break down. The writer of Genesis actually begins to highlight another great story that typifies Christ and the church through the life of Joseph, but that's for another study. This, however, has been the Gospel according to Jacob, the good news according to Genesis 25:21 through Genesis 33:11. For me, this study has unveiled an exquisite masterpiece that has long lain hidden just below the surface of these passages for a time such as this. I hope you too have been able to see the wonderful testimony of Jesus in the story of Jacob.

SIXTEEN

Man Misunderstood

"The light shines in the darkness, but the darkness has not understood it." - John 1:5

Occasionally misunderstandings happen. For years we have seen only glimpses into the revelation presented in this study. We've seen parallels in some of the areas mentioned, but a fuller depth of insight has been missing up to this point for primarily one reason alone; the mislabeling and misunderstanding of a man.

As I've shared this message with people, I'm amazed at the reaction of utter disdain by some toward this God-fearing man, Jacob. The reaction is so different toward King David, who along with being a man after God's heart was also a liar, an adulterer, and a murderer. People love David, but they simply don't like Jacob. This Saturday evening I listened to an evangelist who built his entire message around Jacob, "the deceiver who stole his brother's birthright" being a type of the devil.

Saints of God, we have allowed the reputation of Jacob to cause an otherwise beautiful Scriptural picture of the work of our Savior to go unnoticed for centuries. Jacob's "failures" have loomed large under the microscope of our theological scrutiny to the point of missing who the patriarch Jacob really was and the person he represented.

As we start to wrap up this study, let me briefly address those who are still having a difficult time with Jacob's apparent deception of his father. First of all please remember, Jacob was not perfect. It has not been my intention to paint Jacob as being faultless. Jacob was not Jesus and the parallel I've presented is certainly not perfect. It is only a shadow. In chapter one I mentioned some other commonly accepted Old Testament types of Christ. With only a quick comparison it is easy to find how these accounts fail to perfectly parallel the fuller and more complete work of Christ also. Jonah being in the belly of a fish for three days and three nights was a very different experience from Jesus being three days and three nights in the heart of the earth but yet Jesus used Jonah's event as a picture of what would happen to Him (Matthew 12:40). Abraham offering his son Isaac as a sacrifice is a widely accepted representation of Father God offering His only begotten son Jesus. However, Abraham's account involves a knife, offering Isaac as a burnt offering, an altar, and a ram in the thicket. Of course these elements are not found in Christ's sacrifice, but still it remains a beautiful picture of the Father offering His Son.

The primary purpose of this study has been to look at the picture revealed, not establish if Jacob was justified in doing what he did. As we have seen however, the picture that emerges shows the second-born taking the place of and coming as the firstborn. As we have brought out, this is what Jesus has done for us. For all practical purposes, the full extent of this divine substitution would be virtually impossible to portray without the *appearance* of trickery.

Now, let me attempt for a moment to go beyond our typological study to present some information that is often overlooked when considering the method Jacob used to attain his blessing. This is not an exhaustive list and some of the points have already been mentioned, but let's consider the following:

1. The name Jacob does not mean deceiver nor was it ever intended to mean deceiver by his parents. Jacob was certainly not deceiving Esau at birth. The name Jacob is derived from the Hebrew word for *heel*. Jacob means, "Heel grasper." He was named Jacob simply because he was grabbing his brother's heel.

2. Jacob had already (with no deceit involved) purchased the right to the blessing from his brother. He did not trick or cheat Esau into this very important initial transaction in which all the blessings rested. The blessings belonged to the firstborn and Jacob was legally the firstborn.

Say a father gave a car to his oldest son, but he had to wait until his 21st birthday before he would be given the keys. Sometime before his birthday the young man needed some cash, so he sold his car to his 18-year-old younger brother. When the older brother's 21st birthday rolled around, the father waited in his office to give his firstborn son the keys to the car. What a surprise to the father and disappointment to the older son when the younger son walked in the room.

The blessing Jacob supposedly deceived his father into giving him, already *right*fully belonged to him. It may have taken Isaac off guard, but Jacob was en*titl*ed to it.

In Jacob's dialog with his mother in Genesis 27:12 it says, "What if my father touches me? I would *appear* to be tricking him and would bring down a curse on myself rather than a blessing." Isaac might have thought Jacob was a deceiver since he probably didn't know about what had transpired between Jacob and

Esau. He also probably didn't know that if he had blessed Esau he would have become a hindrance to the promise of God. So, what looked like deception to Isaac due to a limited knowledge of prior events was actually a legitimate exchange. Certainly, from Jacob's statement it seems he didn't view his actions as deception, but rather the receiving of what was *right*fully his. He was going to receive what belonged to him, but he was concerned it would *appear* that he was tricking his father.

3. Jacob was obedient. He obeyed his mother. If Isaac had continued in his plan to bless Esau, he would have falsely prophesied through the blessing pronouncement and would have contradicted the promise of God. Perhaps, if he had involved his (one flesh) wife in his plans, the need for Rebekah to divert a near disaster would have been unnecessary. Also, nowhere in Scripture does God condemn Rebekah for her efforts toward seeing the fulfillment of God's will.

4. God certainly intended Jacob to be the recipient of the promise—*Jacob I loved, Esau I hated.* No alternate means of acquiring the blessing is suggested, nor are the means ever condemned or reversed by Isaac or God. If it were not the appropriate means to secure the blessing, wouldn't God have recorded a rebuke? In fact, just the opposite occurs. God continually reveals Himself to Jacob. God reiterates the promise to him, and blesses him time-and-time again. And, all this takes place *before* his name is changed to Israel and it happens without a single word or hint of correction.

Isn't it also hard to imagine God securing and establishing the rights and blessings of His chosen nation upon an act or acts of deception?

5. Ultimately Jacob was fulfilling the promise given by God—the older would serve the younger. This does not mean the ends justify the means. But, at the same time there are definitely times when God's will and a higher authority must be observed above our conventional understanding.

A few Old Covenant examples may include: God requiring the Israelites to completely destroy the men, women and children of a foreign nation (Deuteronomy 20:16-17). Or, God using the king of Babylon to bring judgment upon Israel (Jeremiah 25:8-9). Or, God using the brazen serpent to represent Jesus, when a serpent traditionally represented the devil (Numbers 21:8-9). Each of these Old Covenant incidents, as well as many others, may be hard to justify *until* greater insight is provided. With greater insight, however, the apparent injustices are reconciled.

A couple New Covenant examples might include: Peter and the other apostles' refusal to obey the religious authorities' restriction to teach in the name of Jesus (Acts 5:28-29). In this case, the apostles were willing to *appear* rebellious in order to be *obedient*.

Another is Peter's vision of unclean animals that he was told to eat and his subsequent ministry to the gentiles (Acts 10). A modern day application may be smuggling Bibles into restricted countries. Should we knowingly "deceptively" attempt to bring banned Bibles or share a banned message in a country where

135

the gospel is not allowed, *or* do you obey God? "Go into all the world and preach the good news to all creation" (Mark 16:15).

6. Isaac told Esau in Genesis 27:35, "Thy brother came with subtilty, and hath taken away thy blessing" (KJV). Subtilty can be translated deceitfully, but it can also carry the connotation of being sly by skill or ingenuity, clever or even having wisdom without necessarily being deceptive or lying. And again, even if Isaac felt tricked, it was most likely because, at the time, he didn't know a transaction had taken place between Jacob and Esau.

7. According to Hebrews 11:20, Isaac dispensed his blessing by faith. Again, it seems, even if Isaac felt tricked, he knew the blessing had somehow been distributed properly and he chose not to revoke it.

8. The argument that Jacob reaped the consequences of his alleged deception by receiving back what he deserved when he lived and worked for Laban, doesn't hold up very long even with a cursory look at the events. Laban was blessed because of Jacob and Jacob ended up getting everything Laban owned. God blessed Jacob everywhere he went and in everything he did, and God doesn't bless deception. He curses and condemns it. Yes, He also forgives, but that's another element that is missing. Nowhere does Scripture indicate that Jacob was ever repentant for what he had done. And yet, God still blesses and communicates with him throughout his life. Perhaps, we should reconsider whether he did anything dishonest.

9. Jacob was a "tam" man. The New International Version interprets "tam" as "quiet" and says that Jacob was a quiet man, staying among the tents (Genesis 25:27). Some believe a more accurate translation for "tam" should be "perfect" or "upright." An alternate rendering would be, "Jacob was an *upright* man, staying among the tents." This seems more appropriate when the entire life and character of Jacob, as well as God's response, interaction, and love for him is considered.

Although Jacob was not perfect in everything he did, at the very least it seems his heart was after God. It also seems that God doesn't mind being associated with him. After all, God continues to reveal Himself as the God of Abraham, Isaac, and *Jacob*.

We can see from these nine points that Jacob being labeled a "swindler" who blatantly deceived his brother and father has possibly been a misunderstanding all along. Perhaps instead of condemning Jacob, Jacob's actions should be viewed as steps of obedience and a desire for the eternal. Not only has the value of Jacob not been grasped, but it also seems to be true that the entire nation of Israel throughout its history has been misunderstood. The misunderstanding and lies that have been attached to Jacob have not remained with him alone. They seem to have been passed on to his offspring in following generations as well. The stereotypes, labels, and misconceptions almost seem deliberate.

Misunderstandings produce fear and opposition. Foreign forces have attempted numerous times to completely annihilate the nation of Israel and the Jewish race from the face of the earth. The existence of Israel has been threatened while in bondage to Egypt, during its wilderness wanderings and in the initial settling of the Promised Land. Israel's survival was also threatened in the rule of judges and during the reign of kings. It was only through divine intervention that Israel became a nation again after being exiled to Persia and Babylon. It was no less miraculous for Israel to have survived the Crusades of the Dark Ages and then again enduring the persecution of the Nazi regime. Misunderstandings produce wars and rumors of wars, but the Truth will always set people free.

One reason we stereotype and generalize people is because it's so much easier than trying to understand them. Generational curses resulting in hatred and persecution start and are perpetuated through the ease of ignorance.

Not only has Jacob and the nation of Israel been misunderstood, but so also has one specific Jewish man named Jesus. Both Jew and gentile have misunderstood Him for some two thousand years. The devil has tried to destroy or at least blanket Jacob/Israel with a cloud of confusion because he ultimately wants to destroy or at least delay the restorative work of Jesus. The devil operates within the ignorance of people to accomplish this task.

Perhaps though, Jesus sovereignly chose to reveal Himself through a man who for years has been labeled with sins he didn't commit, because ultimately, He would bear sins He didn't commit. Perhaps, Jesus chose to reveal Himself through a man who has been mislabeled and a nation that has been misunderstood because He was destined to be a man who would largely go unrecognized Himself. Jesus has been misidentified and misunderstood by the masses. After all, who can understand God? His ways are higher than our ways and His thoughts are higher than our thoughts. Although His ways are higher than our ways, He certainly can relate to you and me when we feel like no one else understands. He's been there.

John 1:5 refers to Jesus being in the world by saying, "The light shines in the darkness, but *the darkness has not understood it.*" This section is titled "Man Misunderstood," and that is exactly what has happened. Man has misunderstood the mission of the Messiah because we've tried to figure everything out before we were willing to receive Him. People won't accept Him until all their questions are answered, and then they may consider Him. But it doesn't work that way. When you turn on a light in a dark room you don't have to understand how the light works before you receive its benefits, you simply receive them. First, we have to receive Jesus, and then He will lead us by His Spirit into all truth. Scientists still don't fully understand the nature of natural light, but someday we will. When we see Him face to face, we will know as He knows and everything will be revealed, but first you have to receive Him.

Once you receive Jesus, it takes some time and a little more effort to get to know Him, but I guarantee its well worth the investment. Truly, the benefits are out of this world. It's time to break the power of ignorance and lies.

God is a God of relationship and He wants you to know Him. God wants the relationship between Him and you to be restored. You may feel like you don't fit in, or like you don't belong, or like no one understands you, but again, I want you to know *Jesus/Jacob* knows exactly how you feel, and He has made it possible for you to become a part of His family.

SEVENTEEN

Jacob Generation

*"But ye are a chosen generation, a royal priesthood, an holy
nation, a peculiar people; that ye should shew forth the praises of
him who hath called you out of darkness into his marvellous light."*
- 1 Peter 2:9 *KJV*

The Esaus of life go into the world hunting wild game with
no regard to the things of God. While their insatiable appetite may
slurp up all the cravings their flesh desires, they remain helpless
and hopeless and will perish unless they receive Jesus. The older
needs the younger in order for the promise to be appropriated. The
younger is the only hope for the older. The world needs Jesus!

The world also has to have a Jacob Generation arise to
reveal this Messiah whom people so desperately need!

I believe the revelation of *Jesus in Jacob* has been brought
to light for such a time as this. I believe it is being released into
the earth because we are nearing the time of the restoration of all
things. It is time for the sons of God to be revealed. The world
groans in eager expectation of it (Romans 8:19-22). *The world is
waiting for you and I to come out of a type and shadows existence
to step into the reality of who we are in Christ.* The world needs
more than a form of godliness. It needs the power of godliness.
It's time for the sons of God to make known the revelation of the
risen Christ.

I believe God is looking for a people in this generation who have a desperate and deep desire for the eternal. God is looking for someone, who despite misunderstanding, threats, and persecution will stand up and serve Him with every fiber of his or her being. Jesus said, "I will give you words and wisdom that none of your adversaries will be able to resist or contradict. You will be betrayed even by parents, brothers, relatives and friends, and they will put some of you to death. All men will hate you because of me. But not a hair of your head will perish. By standing firm you will gain life" (Luke 21:15-19). These people will persevere through hardship and they will overcome!

This generation needs a people who know the power of prayer and realize we are barren without a relationship with Jesus. We need someone who knows how to carry, birth, and impact nations by the power of God. This generation must understand that the Kingdom suffers violence and the violent take it by force (Matthew 11:12).

The world needs those who will give everything they have to gain God and not hold so tightly to the temporary that they forfeit their soul. We need a generation of people who are passionate like Jacob, living beyond the surface in order to live by the Spirit.

The Jacob Generation I'm talking about will fulfill the requirements of the Law by living in and for the Lord. They will be a people of revelation and a people who honor and value their times of intimacy in His presence.

The world needs to be introduced to a people who have been taken hold of and healed by the Lord. We need a host of healed people to stand up today and walk like they've been healed, talk like they've been healed, and tell others how to receive their

142

healing too. We need to be a people who eagerly expect to be used by the Lord and take advantage of each opportunity He presents.

This generation is in desperate need of a people who are tired of their evil twin dominating their day. We need a generation that realizes they are a people of promise and won't settle for a second place fleshly existence. We must realize that we are the church of the firstborn and the gates of hell will not prevail against us!

The world needs you to reach up to God and reach down to snatch those who are perishing from the fire (Jude 23).

The Jacob Generation will go out as sent ones proclaiming the message that Jesus is coming soon; He is coming back to His land and He wants everyone who will to receive the gift that He's provided.

You can be a part of this Jacob Generation. Its time to realize and walk in your firstborn rights by virtue of the Son.

Join the Jacob Generation today as we rise to display the glorious light of the firstborn Son, in whom the Father is well pleased, our Redeemer, our Rock—Jesus Christ the Lord!

TABLE of TYPES

Abraham – type of Father God
Isaac – type of the Spirit God
Rebekah – type of the Justice of God

Esau/Edom - type of Adam (firstborn)(flesh)(fallen mankind)
Jacob/Israel - type of Jesus (second Adam)(the Spirit-led man)
Jacob holding the heel of Esau – type of Jesus holding on to man

Red soup – type of red blood
Two goats – type of scapegoat and sacrificed goat of Lev. 16
Goatskins – type of Jesus coming as a sacrifice
Esau's clothes – type of Jesus putting on humanity
Bread – type of the body
Wine – type of the blood

Rock – type of the church's revelation of Christ
Pouring oil on rock – type of outpouring of Holy Spirit
Rolling stone away from the well – type of the resurrection

Laban – type of the Law
Laban's sons – type of religious leaders
Laban's flock – type of those living under the Law
Laban's idols – type of the traditions of men

Stripes on white within Branch – type of stripes Jesus bore
Spotted and speckled sheep – type of sinful men

Bride – type of the church comprised of both Jew and gentile
Unloved Leah – type of the gentile church
Beloved Rachel – type of Israel, and the Messianic Jew
Jacob saying, "My time is completed." – type of Jesus saying,
"It is finished."

Leah's bridal week – type of the gentile church age
Additional 7 years for Rachel – type of Jacob's Trouble

Jacob wrestling with God – type of Jesus holding on to
the Father's will in the Garden of Gethsemane

Jacob sending gifts ahead of meeting Esau – type of apostles,
prophets, evangelists, pastors and teachers sent before Jesus'
Second Coming

Esau receiving Jacob – man's need to receive Jesus

Jacob saying to Esau that seeing his face was like
seeing the face of God – type of Christians seeing
Jesus face to face at His Second Coming

For information about other study materials
or to have Gary speak at your
church meeting or conference,

go to
infusioncenter.org

e-mail
gmm4j@aol.com

call
864-967-2055

or write:
Gary McInnis
Infusion Worship Center
29 Irish Moss Court
Simpsonville, SC 29680

Made in the USA
Charleston, SC
25 September 2011